Notes On The British Pharmacopoeia

Adolphus Frederick Haselden

Notes on the
British Pharmacopœia.

SHOWING

THE ADDITIONS, OMISSIONS, CHANGE OF NOMENCLATURE, AND
ALTERATIONS, IN THE VARIOUS COMPOUND PREPARATIONS.
WITH THE DOSES OF THOSE MEDICINES WHICH ARE
COMPARATIVELY NEW.

BY

A. F. HASELDEN,

PHARMACEUTICAL CHEMIST,

*Author of a Translation of the Pharmacopœia Londinensis 1836, and of
Papers contributed to the Pharmaceutical Journal.*

LONDON:

ROBERT HARDWICKE, 192, PICCADILLY;
AND ALL BOOKSELLERS.

MDCCCLXIV.

NOTES ON THE

BRITISH PHARMACOPŒIA.

PREFACE.

THE object of the Author in compiling the following pages has been to point out, in a short and simple way, the Additions, Omissions, and Changes of Name which have occurred as regards the British Pharmacopœia when compared with the last Pharmacopœia of London, Edinburgh, and Dublin. In doing this, the Materia Medica Lists have been arranged first, and then those of the Preparations and Compounds. In addition, he has reviewed each preparation separately, and endeavoured to show the actual difference existing between the present and former preparations bearing the same or a similar name, adding such remarks as appeared desirable and likely to be useful; also the dose of those which have been materially altered, or are comparatively new.

To the Appendices he has made some little additions, which he thinks may not be out of place.

The change from troy to avoirdupois weight, affecting the London and Edinburgh Pharmacopœias, should be borne in mind, as also that the grain is unaltered in value.

It only now remains for him to hope that any shortcomings may be excused, and to thank those who have kindly assisted him.

18, CONDUIT STREET, LONDON,
March, 1864.

CONTENTS.

———◆◇◆———

WEIGHTS AND MEASURES.

THE imperial or avoirdupois weight has been adopted for weighing solids in all pharmaceutical preparations, but as there are no subdivisions of the ounce assimilating with those of the fluid ounce, all quantities not answering to the quarter, half or three-quarters of an ounce, are to be signified by grains, there being now no drachm or scruple weights.

The Weights and Measures with their symbols are as follow :—

WEIGHTS.

1 pound	lb. =	16 ounces =	7000 grains.
1 ounce	oz. =	.	= 437.5 grains.
1 grain	gr. =	. —	1 grain.

MEASURES.

1 gallon .	. C	= 8 pints	.	. O viij.
1 pint .	. O	= 20 fluid ounces	.	fl. oz. xx.
1 fluid ounce .	fl. oz.	= 8 fluid drachms		fl. drs. viij.
1 fluid drachm	fl. drm.	= 60 minims	.	. min. lx.
1 minim.	. min.	= 1 minim	.	. min. j.

Temperature in all cases is to be determined by Fahrenheit's thermometer, and the specific gravity of liquids is to be taken at the temperature of 60° (it was 62° before). Liquids are to be measured, unless otherwise directed.

RELATION OF MEASURES TO WEIGHTS OF THE BRITISH
PHARMACOPŒIA.

1 gallon . . = the measure of 10 pounds of water.
1 pint. . .. =   ,,   ,,   1·25   ,,   ,,
1 fluid ounce =   ,,   ,,   1 ounce   ,,
1 fluid drachm =   ,,   ,,   54·68 grains   ,,
1 minim . . =   ,,   ,,   0·91   ,,   ,,

RELATION OF WEIGHTS OF THE BRITISH PHARMACOPŒIA
TO METRICAL WEIGHTS.

1 pound = 453·5925 grammes.
1 ounce = 28·3495   ,,
1 grain =   0·0648   ,,

RELATION OF MEASURES OF THE BRITISH PHARMACOPŒIA
TO METRICAL MEASURES.

1 gallon . . = 4·543487 litres.
1 pint. . . = 0·567936   ,,
1 fluid ounce = 0·028396   ,,
1 fluid drachm = 0·003549   ,,
1 minim . . = 0·000059   ,,

1 litre = one pint, 15 fluid ounces, 1 fluid drachm, and
43·68 minims.

MATERIA MEDICA—ADDITIONS.

Substances contained in the British Pharmacopœia which were not in the last Pharmacopœias.

N. B.—Preparations enumerated in the Materia Medica for which a form is given among Preparations and Compounds, are not noticed in this List.

LONDON.

Acetum Gallicum.
Aqua.
Arnica. Radix.
Balsamum Canadense.
Bela. The half-ripe fruit dried.
Belladonnæ Radix.
Cannabis Indica. The flowering tops of female plant.
Cassia. Pulp.
Chirata. The entire plant.
Cocculus Indicus. The fruit dried.
Conii Fructus.
Cusso. The flowers.
Filix. The rhizome.
Glycerinum.
Hemidesmus. The root dried.
Kamela. Powder adhering to the capsules; chiefly used as a vermifuge.
Laurocerasus. Fresh leaves·
Lini Farina. The seeds ground, the oil being expressed.
Lithiæ Carbonas.
Matica. The dried leaves.
Nectandra. Bark Bebeeru.
Oleum Coriandri.
    „   Cubebæ.
    „   Myristicæ.
    „   Sabinæ.
Plumbi Carbonas.
Podophyllum. The root dried.
Sabadilla. The dried fruit.
Saccharum Lactis.
Santonica.
Scammoniæ Radix.
Spiritus Pyroxylicus Rectificatus.

EDINBURGH.

Aconiti Radix.
Arnica. Radix.
Bela.. The half-ripe fruit dried.
Belladonnæ Radix.
Cannabis Indica. The flowering tops of female plant.
Cerevisiæ Fermentum.
Conii Fructus.
Cusso. The flowers.
Glycerinum.
Hemidesmus. The root dried.
Hirudo.
Kamela. Powder adhering to the capsules; chiefly used as a vermifuge.
Lithiæ Carbonas.
Matica. The dried leaves.
Mori Succus.
Nectandra. Bark Bebeeru.
Oleum Amygdalæ.
„   Anethi.
Oleum Anisi.
„   Anthemidis.
„   Carui.
„   Caryophylli.
„   Cinnamomi.
„   Coriandri.
„   Cubebæ.
„   Menthæ Viridis.
„   Morrhuæ.
„   Pimentæ.
„   Rosmarini.
„   Sabinæ.
Saccharum Lactis.
Santonica.
Scammoniæ Radix.
Spiritus Pyroxylicus Rectificatus.
Stramonii Semina.
Terebinthina Canadensis.
Thus.
Ulmus.

DUBLIN.

Aconitum. Leaves and flowering tops.
Aloe Barbadensis.
Anethum. The fruit.
Armoracia. Fresh root.
Arnica. Radix.
Aqua Aurantii. From the flowers.
Balsamum Peruvianum.
Bela. The half-ripe fruit dried.
Cambogia. Siam.
Cassia. Pulp.
Cocculus Indicus. The fruit dried.
Conii Fructus.
Cusparia.
Cusso. The flowers.
Filix. The rhizome.
Kamela. Powder adhering to the capsules; chiefly used as a vermifuge.
Kino Malabar.
Lini Farina. The seeds ground, the oil being expressed.
Lithiæ Carbonas.
Mori Succus.
Myristicæ Adeps. The concrete oil.

Nectandra. Bark Bebeeru.
Oleum Amygdalæ.
    „   Anethi.
    „   Anisi.
    „   Anthemidis.
    „   Cajuputi.
    „   Carui.
    „   Caryophylli.
    „   Cinnamomi.
    „   Copaibæ.
    „   Coriandri.
    „   Cubebæ.
    „   Juniperi.
    „   Lavandulæ.
    „   Limonis.
    „   Menthæ Piperitæ.
    „   Menthæ Viridis.
    „   Myristicæ.

Oleum Pimentæ.
    „   Rosmarini.
    „   Rutæ.
    „   Sabinæ.
Podophyllum. The root dried.
Pterocarpus. Wood.
Rosa Canina. The ripe fruit deprived of the hairy seeds.
Sabadilla. The dried fruit.
Sambucus. The fresh flowers.
Santonica.
Sapo Mollis.
Scammoniæ Radix.
Sevum Præparatum.
Stramonii Folia.
Styrax Præparatus.
Terebinthina Canadensis.
Ulmus.

MATERIA MEDICA—OMISSIONS.

Substances omitted in the British Pharmacopœia which were contained in the last Pharmacopœias.

LONDON.

Absinthium.
Acetum Britannicum.
Ærugo.
Althæa.
Aloe Hepatica.
Anisum.
Antimonii Tersulphuretum.
Aqua Destillata.
Avena.
Bismuthum.
Calamina Præparata.
Calcii Chloridum.
Canella.
Carota.
Cassia Fruit.
Chimaphila.
Cornu.
Cornu Ustum.
Cydonium.
Cyminum.
Elaterium. Fructus.
Farina.
Ferrum in fila tractum.
Fœniculi Oleum.
Granatum. Fructûs Cortex.
Helleborus.

Hydrargyrum.
Juniperus.
Lactuca.
Laurus.
Manganesii Binoxidum.
Maranta.
Mentha Piperita.
  „   Viridis.
Morphiæ Acetas.
Mucuna.
Ovi Albumen.
  „ Vitellus.
Panis.
Petroleum.
Phosphorus.
Piper Longum.
Pix.
Potassii Ferrocyanidum.
Pulegium.
Pulegii Oleum.
Pyrethrum.
Rhamni Succus.
Ruta.
Sagapenum.
Sago.
Silex Contritus.

Sodæ Sulphas.
Spiritus Tenuior.
   „   Vini Gallici.
Staphisagria.
Terebinthina (Americana).

Tormentilla.
Veratrum.
Viola.
Zincum.

EDINBURGH.

Absinthium.
Acetum Britannicum.
   „   Destillatum.
Ærugo.
Alcohol.
Allium.
Aloe Indica.
Althææ Folia et Radix.
Ammoniæ Spiritus.
Amygdala Amara.
Angelica.
Anisum.
Antimonii Tersulphuretum.
Aqua Destillata.
Argentum.
Aurantii Oleum.
Avena.
Barytæ Carbonas.
   „   Murias.
   „   Sulphas.
Bergamotæ Oleum.
Bismuthum.
Calamina Præparata.
Calamus Aromaticus.
Calcis Murias.
Cambogia Zeylanica.
Canella.
Canna.
Cassiæ Cortex.
   „   Oleum.
Centaurium.
Cinchona Cinerea.
Cinnabaris.

Cornu.
Creta.
Cuminum.
Cuprum Ammoniatum.
Curcuma.
Dauci Radix.
Euphorbium.
Farina.
Ferri Filum.
   „   Limatura.
   „   Sulphuretum.
Gossypium.
Helleborus.
Juniperi Cacumina.
   „   Fructus.
Lacmus.
Lactucarium.
Lavandula.
Linum Catharticum.
Malva.
Manganesii Oxydum.
Maranta.
Marmor.
Melissa.
Mentha Piperita.
   „   Viridis.
Menyanthes.
Morphiæ Acetas.
Mucuna.
Origanum.
Ovum.
Petroleum.
Piper Longum.

Pix Arida.
Plumbi Iodidum.
„   Nitras.
„   Oxydum Rubrum.
Potassa cum Calce.
Potassæ Aqua Effervescens.
„   Bisulphas.
„   Sulphas cum Sul-
       phure.
Potassii Ferrocyanidum.
Pulegium.
Pyrethrum.
Pyrola.
Rhamni Baccæ.
Rosæ Oleum.
Rosmarinus.
Ruta.

Saccharum Commune.
Sago.
Salicis Cortex.
Simaruba.
Sodæ Aqua Effervescens.
„   Sulphas.
Spigelia.
Spongia.
Stannum.
Staphisagria.
Tapioca.
Terebinthina Chia.
„   Veneta.
Tormentilla.
Veratrum.
Viola.
Zincum.

DUBLIN.

Ærugo.
Aloe Hepatica.
Anisum.
Antimonii Sulphuretum.
Argentum Purificatum.
Avena Sativa.
Barytæ Carbonas.
„   Sulphas.
Bismuthum.
Calcis Carbonas.
Canella Alba.
Canna Edulis.
Chimaphila Umbellata.
Cinchona Micrantha.
Citrus Aurantium.
Cupri Subacetas.
Cycas Circinalis.
Daucus Carota.
Dolichos.
Farina.
Ferrum.

Hebradendron Gambogioides.
Janipha Manihot.
Juniperus Communis.
Lactuca Sativa.
„   Virosa.
Lactucarium.
Lavandula Vera.
Lixivus Cinis.
Manganesii Peroxidum.
Maranta Arundinacea.
Marmor Album.
Mentha Piperita.
„   Pulegium.
„   Viridis.
Mucuna Pruriens.
Oleum Rosæ.
Ossa.
Ovum.
Pimpinella Anisum.
Potassæ Bichromas.
Potassii Ferrocyanidum.

Pterocarpus Erinaceus.
Pulegium.
Pyrola.
Rosmarinus Officinalis.
Saccharum Officinarum.
Sago.
Simaruba Amara.

Sodæ Sulphas.
Stannum.
Succinum.
Tapioca.
Triticum Æstivum.
Zincum.

MATERIA MEDICA.

Substances, the Names of which have been Changed.

FORMER NAME.	PRESENT NAME.
E. Acidum Aceticum	Acidum Aceticum Glaciale.
E. ,, Muriaticum	,, Hydrochloricum.
E. ,, Pyroligneum	,, Aceticum.
L. Aconiti Folium	Aconitum.
L. Adeps	⎫
E. Axungia	⎬ Adeps Præparatus.
D. Adeps Suillus	⎭
E. Æther Sulphuricus	Æther.
D. Agathotes Chirayita	Chirata.
E. Ammoniæ Murias	⎫ Ammoniæ Hydrochloras.
D. ,, ,,	⎭
L. ,, Sesquicarbonas	⎫ Ammoniæ Carbonas.
D. ,, ,,	⎭
E. Amygdala Dulcis	⎫ Amygdala.
D. Amygdalus Communis	⎭
E. Arsenicum Album	Acidum Arseniosum.
E. Balsamum Canadense	Terebinthina Canadensis.
L. Buchu	⎫
E. Bucku	⎬ Bucco.
D. Barosma Crenata	⎭
L. Calx Chlorinata	⎫
E. ,, ,,	⎬ Calx Chlorata.
D. ,, ,,	⎭
L. Catechu. Acacia Catechu ligni interioris Extractum	⎫
E. Catechu ,,	⎬ Catechu Nigrum.
D. ,, ,,	⎭
L. ,, Uncaria Gambir	⎫
E. ,, ,, ,,	⎬ Catechu Pallidum.
D. ,, ,, ,,	⎭

FORMER NAME.	PRESENT NAME.
L. Cera - - - -	Cera Flava.
E. Chiretta - - - -	Chirata.
E. Cinchona Coronæ -	Cinchona Pallida.
L. Guaiacum - - - ⎫	
E. „ - - - ⎬	Guaiaci Resina.
D. Glycerina - - -	Glycerinum.
E. Gummi Acaciæ - -	Acacia.
D. Humulus - - -	Lupulus.
D. Iodinium - - - -	Iodum.
L. Myristicæ Oleum -	Myristicæ Adeps.
D. Myristica Moschata -	Myristica.
L. Piper Nigrum - - -	Piper.
L. Plumbi Oxidum - -	Lithargyrum.
L. Potassæ Bitartras - ⎫	
E. „ „ - ⎬	Potassæ Tartras Acida.
D. „ „ - ⎭	
L. Potassii Sulphuretum ⎫	
E. „ „ - ⎬	Potassa Sulphurata.
L. Sacchari Fæx - - ⎫	
E. „ „ - ⎬	Theriaca.
L. Sapo - - - -	Sapo Durus.
L. Sevum - - - -	Sevum Præparatum.
E. Sodæ Murias - - -	Sodii Chloridum.
L. Sulphur - - - ⎫	
E. „ - - - ⎬	Sulphur Sublimatum.
L. Tiglii Oleum - - -	Crotonis Oleum.

PREPARATIONS AND COMPOUNDS.

ADDITIONS.

Preparations, the Form for which was not given in the last Pharmacopœias as marked.

	E.		Acidum Aceticum Dilutum.
L.	E.		„ „ Glaciale.
L.	E.		„ Arseniosum.
L.			„ Benzoicum.
L.		D.	„ Citricum.
L.	E.		„ Gallicum.
L.			„ Hydrochloricum.
L.			„ Nitricum.
L.	E.	D.	„ Nitro-Hydrochloricum Dilutum.
	E.	D.	„ Phosphoricum Dilutum.
L.			„ Sulphuricum Aromaticum.
L.	E.	D.	„ Sulphurosum.
L.	E.		„ Tannicum.
L.		D.	„ Tartaricum.
L.	E.	D.	Aconitia.
L.	E.		Adeps Præparatus.
L.			Æther.
L.	E.	D.	Ammoniæ Benzoas.
L.	E.	D.	„ Phosphas.
L.			Antimonii Oxidum.
		D.	Aqua Anethi.
L.			„ Fœniculi.
L.			„ Laurocerasi.
		D.	„ Sambuci.
L.	E.		Argenti Oxidum.

L. E. D. Atropia.
L. E. D. Beberiæ Sulphas.
L. E.   Calcis Carbonas Præcipitata.
L. E. D.   „   Hydras.
L. E.   „   Phosphas Præcipitata.
L.   Carbo-Animalis Purificatus.
   E. D. Cataplasma Carbonis.
   E. D.   „   Conii.
   E. D.   „   Fermenti.
   E. D.   „   Lini.
   E. D.   „   Sinapis.
   E. D.   „   Sodæ Chloratæ.
   E.   Chloroformum.
L. E. D. Collodium.
     D. Confectio Rosæ Caninæ.
   E.   „   Scammonii.
L. E.   „   Sulphuris.
L. E.   „   Terebinthinæ.
L.   Creta Præparata.
   E. D. Cupri Sulphas.
   E.   Decoctum Cetrariæ.
     D.   „   Cinchonæ Flavæ.
   E. D.   „   Granati Radicis.
   E. D.   „   Pareiræ.
     D.   „   Taraxaci.
L. E. D. Digitalinum.
L. E.   Emplastrum Calefaciens.
     D.   „   Galbani.
     D.   „   Picis.
   E. D. Enema Aloes.
L.   „   Magnesiæ Sulphatis.
     D. Extractum Aconiti.
   E. D.   „   Aloes Barbadensis.
   E. D.   „   „   Socotrinæ.
L. E. D.   „   Belæ Liquidum.
L. E. D.   „   Calumbæ.
L. E.   „   Cannabis Indicæ.
   E. D.   „   Cinchonæ Flavæ Liquidum.
   E. D.   „   Colchici.
   E. D.   „   Colocynthidis Compositum.
L. E. D.   „   Ergotæ Liquidum.
L. E. D.   „   Filicis Liquidum.
     D.   „   Hæmatoxyli.
     D.   „   Jalapæ.

L.		D.	Extractum Krameriæ.
		D.	,, Lupuli.
		D.	,, Nucis Vomicæ.
L.	E.	D.	,, Opii Liquidum.
L.	E.	D.	,, Pareiræ Liquidum.
L.		D.	,, Quassiæ.
		D.	,, Stramonii.
		D.	,, Taraxaci.
L.	E.	D.	Fel Bovinum Purificatum.
L.	E.	D.	Ferri Arsenias.
	E.		,, et Ammoniæ Citras.
L.	E.	D.	,, et Quiniæ Citras.
L.			,, Iodidum.
L.			,, Oxidum Magneticum.
L.	E.		,, Peroxidum Hydratum.
L.	E.	D.	,, Phosphas.
L.	E.		,, Sulphas Granulata.
L.			,, ., Exsiccata.
L.	E.		Ferrum Redactum.
L.			Hydrargyri Iodidum Rubrum.
	E.		,, ,, Viride.
L.	E.		Hydrargyrum.
L.			Infusum Chiratæ.
		D.	,, Cuspariæ.
L.	E.	D.	,, Cusso.
L.	E.	D.	,, Dulcamaræ.
L.	E.		,, Ergotæ.
	E.		,, Krameriæ.
	E.	D.	,, Lupuli.
L.	E.		,, Maticæ.
L.			,, Senegæ.
		D.	,, Serpentariæ.
L.	E.	D.	,, Uvæ Ursi.
	E.		,, Valerianæ.
L.		D.	Iodum.
L.		D.	Jalapæ Resina.
L.	E.	D.	Linimentum Aconiti.
L.	E.	D.	,, Belladonnæ.
L.	E.	D.	,, Cantharidis.
L.	E.	D.	,, Chloroformi.
L.	E.		,, Crotonis.
L.	E.	D.	,, Iodi.
L.	E.	D.	,, Terebinthinæ Aceticum.

L.	E.		Liquor Antimonii Terchloridi.
L.	E.	D.	,, Atropiæ.
L.	E.	D.	,, Calcis Saccharatus.
L.	E.	D.	,, Ferri Perchloridi.
L.	E.	D.	,, Hydrargyri Nitratis Acidus.
L.	E.	D.	,, Potassæ Permanganatis.
	E.		,, Sodæ.
L.	E.	D.	,, ,, Arseniatis.
L.	E.	D.	,, Strychniæ.
L.	E.	D.	Lithiæ Citras.
L.	E.		Mel Depuratum. ,
	E.		Mistura Ammoniaci.
L.		D.	,, Creasoti.
		D.	,, Guaiaci.
L.		D.	,, Scammonii.
L.			Morphiæ Hydrochloras.
	E.		Mucilago Amyli.
L.		D.	,, Tragacanthæ.
	E.		Oxymel.
L.	E.	D.	Pilula Aloes Barbadensis.
L.		D.	,, Aloes et Assafœtidæ.
L.		D.	,, Aloes Socotrinæ.
L.			,, Assafœtidæ Composita.
	E.		,, Cambogiæ Composita.
L.			,, Colocynthidis ,,
L.		D.	,, ,, et Hyoscyami.
L.	E.		,, Ferri Carbonatis.
L.	E.	D.	,, ,, Iodidi.
L.		D.	,, Plumbi cum Opio.
L.		D.	Plumbi Acetas.
L.	E.	D.	Podophylli Resina.
L.			Potassa Sulphurata.
L.			Potassæ Bicarbonas.
L.	E.	D.	,, Chloras.
L.	E.	D.	,, Citras.
L.	E.		,, Nitras.
L.	E.	D.	,, Permanganas.
L.			,, Sulphas.
L.			,, Tartras.
L.	E.	D.	Potassii Bromidum.
L.			,, Iodidum.
		D.	Pulvis Amygdalæ Compositus.
L.		D.	,, Catechu Compositus.

	E.	D.	Pulvis Cretæ Aromaticus.	
L.	E.	D.	„ „ „ cum Opio.	
	E.	D.	„ Kino Compositus.	
L.			„ Rhei Compositus.	
		D.	„ Tragacanthæ „	
L.			Quiniæ Sulphas.	
L.	E.	D.	Santoninum.	
L.	E.	D.	Scammoniæ Resina.	
L.	E.	D.	Soda Caustica.	
L.	E.	D.	Sodæ Arsenias.	
L.			„ Bicarbonas.	
L.	E.		„ et Potassæ Tartras.	
L.			„ Phosphas.	
L.		D.	Spiritus Ætheris.	
	E.	D.	„ Armoraciæ Compositus.	
L.	E.	D.	„ Cajuputi.	
L.	E.	D.	„ Chloroformi.	
L.		D.	„ Lavandulæ.	
	E.	D.	„ Menthæ Piperitæ.	
		D.	„ Myristicæ.	
		D.	„ Rosmarini.	
L.			Strychnia.	
L.	E.	D.	Succus Conii.	
L.	E.	D.	„ Scoparii.	
L.	E.	D.	„ Taraxaci.	
L.	E.	D.	Sulphur Præcipitatum.	
L.	E.	D.	Suppositoria Acidi Tannici.	
L.	E.	D.	„ Morphiæ.	
L.	E.	D.	Syrupus Aurantii Floris.	
	E.		„ Ferri Iodidi.	
L.	E.	D.	„ „ Phosphatis.	
L.	E.		„ Hemidesmi.	
		D.	„ Limonis.	
	E.	D.	„ Mori.	
		D.	„ Papaveris.	
		D.	„ Rhœados.	
L.			„ Rosæ Gallicæ.	
L.			„ Scillæ.	
		D.	„ Sennæ.	
	E.		Tinctura Aconiti.	
		D.	„ Aloes.	
L.	E.	D.	„ Arnicæ.	
	E.		„ Belladonnæ.	
		D.	„ Benzoini Composita.	

L.			Tinctura Bucco.
L.	E.		„ Cannabis Indicæ.
		D.	„ Castorei.
L.	E.		„ Chiratæ.
		D.	„ Cinnamomi.
L.	E.	D.	„ Conii Fructus.
L.			„ Croci.
L.	E.		„ Ergotæ.
		D.	„ Guaiaci Ammoniata.
		D.	„ Kino.
L.	E.		„ Krameriæ.
	E.		„ Limonis.
		D.	„ Lobeliæ Ætherea.
L.	E.	D.	„ Nucis Vomicæ.
	E.	D.	„ Quiniæ Composita.
L.	E.	D.	„ Sabinæ.
L.	E.	D.	„ Senegæ.
		D.	„ Serpentariæ.
L.	E.		„ Stramonii.
		D.	„ Valerianæ Ammoniatæ.
L.	E.	D.	Trochisci Acidi Tannici.
L.	E.	D.	„ Bismuthi.
L.	E.	D.	„ Catechu.
L.		D.	„ Morphiæ.
L.		D.	„ „ et Ipecacuanhæ.
L.		D.	„ Opii.
L.	E.	D.	Unguentum Aconitiæ.
L.	E.	D.	„ Atropiæ.
	E.	D.	„ Belladonnæ.
L.	E.	D.	„ Calomelanos.
	E.		„ Cetacei.
L.		D.	„ Cocculi.
	E.		„ Elemi.
L.	E.		„ Gallæ.
		D.	„ „ cum Opio.
		D.	„ Hydrargyri Ammoniati.
L.	E.		„ „ Iodidi Rubri.
L.			„ Plumbi Carbonatis.
	E.		„ Potassii Iodidi.
L.		D.	„ Simplex.
L.	E.	D.	„ Terebinthinæ.
L.	E.	D.	„ Veratriæ.
L.		D.	Veratria.
		D.	Vinum Aloes.

			Vinum Antimoniale.
		D.	Vinum Antimoniale.
		D.	„ Colchici.
	E.	D.	„ Ferri.
L.	E.		Zinci Acetas.
L.	E.		„ Carbonas.
	E.		„ Chloridum.
L.	E.		„ Valerianas.

PREPARATIONS AND COMPOUNDS.

OMISSIONS.

Preparations omitted in the British Pharmacopœia which were contained in the last Pharmacopœias, as follows :

LONDON.

Acetum Destillatum.
„ Cantharidis.
„ Colchici.
„ Scillæ.
Ammoniacum Præparatum.
Assafœtida Præparata.
Aqua Pulegii.
Atropiæ Sulphas.
Cassia Præparata.
Ceratum.
„ Calaminæ.
„ Cantharidis.
„ Cetacei.
„ Hydrargyri Compositum.
„ Plumbi Acetatis.
„ „ Compositum.
„ Resinæ.
„ Saponis Compositum.
Confectio Aurantii.
„ Cassiæ.
„ Opii.
„ Rutæ.
Cupri Ammonio-Sulphas.
Decoctum Amyli.

Decoctum Chimaphilæ.
„ Cinchonæ Pallidæ.
„ „ Rubræ.
„ Cydonii.
„ Dulcamaræ.
„ Gallæ.
„ Granati.
„ Hordei Compositum.
„ Senegæ.
„ Ulmi.
„ Tormentillæ.
„ Uvæ Ursi.
Emplastrum Ammoniaci.
„ Cumini.
„ Potassii Iodidi.
Enema Colocynthidis.
Extractum Cinchonæ.
„ „ Pallidæ.
„ „ Rubræ.
„ Colocynthidis.
„ Lactucæ.
„ Papaveris.
„ Pareiræ.
„ Uvæ Ursi.

Ferri Ammonio-Chloridum.
Galbanum Præparatum.
Hydrargyri Bisulphuretum.
Infusum Armoraciæ Compositum.
    „   Aurantii   „
    „   Cinchonæ Pallidæ.
Linimentum Æruginis.
    „   Ammoniæ Sesquicarbonatis.
Liquor Ammoniæ Citratis.
    „   „   Sesquicarbonatis.
    „   Aluminis Compositus.
    „   Arsenici Chloridi.
    „   Cupri Ammonio-Sulphatis.
    „   Hydrargyri Bichloridi.
    „   Morphiæ Acetatis.
    „   Potassæ Carbonatis.
    „   Potassii Iodidi.
Mel Rosæ.
Mistura Gentianæ Composita.
    „   Spiritus Vini Gallici.
Oleum Æthereum.
Oxymel Scillæ.
Pilula Aloes Composita.
    „   „ cum Sapone.
    „   Conii Composita.
    „   Ferri Composita.
    „   Galbani Composita.
    „   Ipecacuanhæ cum Scillâ
    „   Styracis Composita.
Pix Burgundica Præparata.
Plumbi Iodidum.
Potassa cum Calce.
Prunum Præparatum.
Pulvis Aloes Compositus.
    „   Cinnamomi Compositus.
    „   Cretæ Compositus.
    „   „   „ cum Opio.

Sagapenum Præparatum.
Spiritus Ammoniæ Fœtidus.
    „   Anisi.
    „   Carui.
    „   Cinnamomi.
    „   Pimentæ.
    „   Pulegii.
Sulphuris Iodidum.
Syrupus Althææ.
    „   Cocci.
    „   Croci.
    „   Rhamni.
    „   Rosæ.
    „   Sarsæ.
    „   Violæ
Tamarindus Præparatus.
Thus Præparatum.
Tinctura Aloes Composita.
    „   Ammoniæ „
    „   Cinchonæ Pallidæ.
    „   Cinnamomi Composita.
    „   Colchici Composita.
    „   Conii.
    „   Cubebæ.
    „   Ergotæ Ætherea.
    „   Ferri Ammonio-Chloridi.
    „   Hellebori.
Unguentum Conii.
    „   Hydrargyri Nitratis Mitius.
    „   Opii.
    „   Picis.
    „   Picis Liquidæ.
    „   Plumbi Compositum.
    „   Plumbi Iodidi.
    „   Sambuci.
    „   Sulphuris Compositum.
    „   Sulphuris Iodidi.
Vinum Veratri.

EDINBURGH.

Acetum Cantharidis.
" Colchici.
" Destillatum.
" Opii.
" Scillæ.
Acidum Aceticum Camphoratum.
Aqua Cassiæ.
" Pulegii.
" Potassæ Effervescens.
" Sodæ "
Barii Chloridum.
Calcii "
Calx.
Cassia Præparata.
Ceratum Calaminæ.
" Simplex.
Cupri Ammonio-Sulphas.
Decoctum Dulcamaræ.
" Guaiaci.
" Scoparii Compositum.
Electuarium Aromaticum.
" Catechu.
" Opii.
Emplastrum Ammoniaci.
" Assafœtidæ.
" Cantharidis Compositum.
" Simplex.
Extractum Colocynthidis.
" Digitalis.
" Papaveris.
" Pareiræ.
" Scammonii.
Ferri Sulphuretum.
Hydrargyri "
Infusum Pareiræ.
" Simarubæ.
Linimentum Ammoniæ Compositum.

Linimentum Simplex.
Liquor Ammoniæ Sesquicarbonatis.
" Cupri Ammonio-Sulphatis.
" Potassii Iodidi Compositus.
Mel Rosæ.
Mistura Acaciæ.
" Althææ.
" Camphoræ cum Magnesia.
" Hordei.
Morphiæ Acetas.
Oleum Copaibæ.
" Terebinthinæ Purificatum.
Pilula Cupri Ammoniati.
" Ferri Sulphatis.
" Hydrargyri et Opii.
" Ipecacuanhæ et Opii.
" Rhei.
" Rhei et Ferri.
" Styracis Composita.
Plumbi Iodidum.
" Nitras.
Potassa cum Calce.
Potassæ Bisulphas.
" Carbonas.
" Sulphuretum cum Sulphure.
Pulvis Effervescens.
" Aluminis Compositus.
" Cinnamomi "
" Cretæ "
" Salinus "
Sodæ Sulphas.
Spiritus Ætheris Compositus.
" Ammoniæ.
" " Fœtidus.
" Carui.

Spiritus Cassiæ.
„   Cinnamomi.
„   Juniperi Compositus.
Stanni Pulvis.
Syrupus Aceti.
„   Althææ.
„   Croci.
„   Ipecacuanhæ.
„   Rhamni.
„   Rosæ.
„   Sarsæ.
„   Violæ.
Tinctura Aloes Composita.
„   Cardamomi.
„   Cassiæ.
„   Cinnamomi   Com-
          posita.
„   Cuspariæ.
„   Guaiaci.
„   Conii.

Tinctura Lactucarii.
„   Opii Ammoniata.
„   Quassiæ.
„   „   Composita.
„   Rhei et Aloes.
„   „   Gentianæ.
Trochisci Acaciæ.
„   Cretæ.
„   Glycyrrhizæ.
„   Magnesiæ.
„   Lactucarii.
„   Sodæ Bicarbonatis.
Unguentum Æruginis.
„   Infusi Canthari-
          dis.
„   Picis Liquidæ.
Vinum Gentianæ.
„   Rhei.
„   Tabaci.

DUBLIN.

Acetum Cantharidis.
„   Colchici.
„   Scillæ.
„   Opii.
Acidum Aceticum Camphora-
    tum.
Alcohol Amylicum.
Ammoniæ   Hydro-Sulphure-
    tum.
Antimonii Sulphuretum Præ-
    cipitatum.
Aqua Anisi.
Arsenicum Purum.
Calcis Carbonas Præcipitatum.
Confectio Catechu Composi-
    tum.
Creta Præparata.
Cupri Ammonio-Sulphas.
    Subacetas Præparatum.

Decoctum Dulcamaræ.
„ - Cinchonæ Pallidæ.
„   Lini Compositum.
„   Myrrhæ.
„   Pyrolæ.
„   Uvæ Ursi.
Emplastrum Ammoniaci.
Ferri Valerianas.
Hepar Sulphuris.
Hydrargyrum cum Magnesiâ.
Hydrargyri Sulphas.
Infusum Aurantii Compositum
„   Cinchonæ Pallidæ.
„   Juniperi.
„   Menthæ Viridis.
„   Pareiræ.
„   Simarubæ.
Liquor Arsenici et Hydrar-
    gyri Hydriodatis.

Liquor Antimonii Tartarizati.
,, Barii Chloridi.
,, Calcii Chloridi.
,, Morphiæ Acetatis.
,, Potassæ Carbonatis.
,, Potassii Iod. Compos.
,, Sodæ Carbonatis.
,, Zinci Chloridi.
Mistura Ferri Aromatica.
Morphia.
Morphiæ Acetas.
Mucilago Hordei.
Pilula Aloes Composita.
,, Saponis ,,
Plumbi Iodidum.
,, Nitras.
Potassæ Bisulphas.
,, Carbonas Purum.
Potassa Caustica cum Calce.
Pulvis Cretæ Compositus.
,, ,, Opiatus.
Pulveres Effervescentes Citrati.
,, Effervescentes Tartarizati.

Quinæ Murias.
,, Valerianas.
Sodæ Acetas.
Spiritus Æthereus Oleosus.
,, Fortior.
,, Ammoniæ Fœtidus.
Strychniæ Murias.
Stanni Pulvis.
Sulphur Iodatum.
Syrupus Acidi Citrici.
,, Croci.
,, Morphiæ Acetatis.
,, ,, Muriatis.
Tinctura Cinnamomi Composita.
,, Cubebæ.
,, Ferri Acetatis.
,, Guaiaci.
,, Matico.
Unguentum Ceræ Albæ.
,, Cupri Subacetatis.
,, Picis Liquidæ.
,, Plumbi Iodidi.
Vinum Rhei.

PREPARATIONS AND COMPOUNDS

OF WHICH THE NAMES HAVE BEEN

CHANGED.

———◇◇◇———

FORMER NAME.	PRESENT NAME.
Aconitina - - -	Aconitia.
E. Ammoniæ Acetatis Aqua -	Liquor Ammoniæ Acetatis.
L. Antimonii Oxysulphure- tum. E. „ Sulphuretum Aureum. D. „ Sulphuretum Præcipitatum.	Antimonium Sulphuratum.
L. „ Potassio-Tartras E. Antimonium Tartarizatum D. „ „	Antimonium Tartaratum.
E. Aqua Ammoniæ - -	Liquor Ammoniæ.
E. Aqua Chlorinei - -	Aqua Chlori.
E. Aqua Ammoniæ Fortior -	Liquor Ammoniæ Fortior.
E. Aqua Potassæ - - -	Liquor Potassæ.
L. Bismuthi Nitras - - D. „ Subnitras - -	Bismuthum Album.
L. Cataplasma Sodæ Chlori- natæ.	Cataplasma Sodæ Chloratæ.
L. Chloroformyl - - - E. „ - - - D. „ - - -	Chloroformum.
L. Confectio Amygdalæ - E. Conserva „ -	Pulvis Amygdalæ Compo- situs.
L. Confectio Aromatica -	Pulvis Cretæ Aromaticus.
D. Confectio Piperis Nigri - E. Electuarium Piperis - -	Confectio Piperis.
L. Decoctum Amyli - -	Mucilago Amyli.
L. Emplastrum Plumbi - -	Emplastrum Lithargyri.

FORMER NAME.	PRESENT NAME.
E. Enema Catharticum - - D. ,, ,, -	} EnemaMagnesiæSulphatis.
D. Essentia Menthæ Piperitæ	Spiritus Menthæ Piperitæ.
D. ,, Myristicæ Mos- chatæ.	} ,, Myristicæ.
D. ,, Rosmarini - -	,, Rosmarini.
L. Extractum Aloes - - D. ,, Aloes Aquosum	} Extractum Aloes Socotrinæ.
D. ,, Cannabis Indicæ Purificatum.	} ,, Cannabis Indicæ.
E. Ferri Oxidum Nigrum -	Ferri Oxidum Magneticum.
L. Ferri Sesquioxydum - E. ,, Oxidum Rubrum -	} Ferri Peroxidum.
D. ,, Pulvis - -	Ferrum Redactum.
L. ,, Potassio-Tartras -	
E. Ferrum Tartarizatum - D. ,, ,, -	} Ferrum Tartaratum.
L. Hydrargyri Chloridum - L. ,, Ammonio- Chloridum.	Calomelas.

E. Hydrargyrum Præcipita-
         tum Album.
 D. Hydrargyri   Ammonio-
           Chloridum.
	Hydrargyrum Ammoniatum.

L. ,, Bichloridum -	} Hydrargyrum Corrosivum Sublimatum.
E. ,, Biniodidum -	HydrargyriIodidumRubrum
L. ,, Iodidum -	,, ,, Viride.
L. ,, Nitrico-oxidum	,, Oxidum Rubrum.
L. Infusum Cinchonæ Spissa- tum.	} Extractum Cinchonæ Flavæ Liquidum.
L. ,, Buchu - - E. ,, ,, - - D. ,, ,, - -	} Infusum Bucco.
L. ,, Catechu Composi- tum. D. ,, ,, ,,	} ,, Catechu.
L. ,, Cinchonæ - - E. ,, ,, - -	} ,, Cinchonæ Flavæ.
L. ,, Lini Compositum	,, Lini.
L. ,, Rosæ ,, E. ,, Rosæ - -	} ,, Rosæ Acidum.

FORMER NAME.	PRESENT NAME.
L. Infusum Sennæ Compositum.	} Infusum Sennæ.
D. ,, ,, ,,	
E. Iodinium - - - -	} Iodum.
D. ,, Purum - -	
D. Liquor Antimonii Tartarizati.	} Vinum Antimoniale.
D. ,, Calcis Chlorinatæ -	Liquor Calcis Chloratæ.
L. ,, Chlorinii - -	} Aqua Chlori.
D. ,, ,, - -	
D. ,, Hydrargyri Pernitratis.	} Liquor Hydrargyri Nitratis Acidus.
L. ,, Plumbi Diacetatis -	,, Plumbi Subacetatis.
L. ,, ,, Dilutus.	} ,,Dilutus. ,, ,,
D. ,, ,, Subacetatis Compositus.	,, ,, ,,
L. ,, Sodæ Chlorinatæ	} Liquor Sodæ Chloratæ.
D. ,, ,, ,,	
L. Magnesia - - -	
E. ,, - - -	} Magnesia Levis.
D. ,, - - -	
L. ,, Carbonas -	
E. ,, ,,	} Magnesiæ Carbonas Levis.
D. ,, ,,	
D. ,, ,, Ponderosum	} Magnesiæ Carbonas.
L. Mistura Camphoræ -	} Aqua Camphoræ.
D. ,, ,,	
L. ,, Acaciæ -	} Mucilago Acaciæ.
E. Mucilago - - -	
E. Morphiæ Murias -	} Morphiæ Hydrochloras.
D. ,, ,,	
L. Pilula Hydrargyri Chloridi Composita -	} Pilula Calomelanos Composita.
E. ,, Cambogiæ -	Pilula Cambogiæ Composita.
L. ,, Saponis Composita	} ,, Opii.
D. ,, ,, ,,	
E. ,, Plumbi Opiata -	Pilula Plumbi cum Opio.
E. Plumbi Diacetatis Solutio	Liquor Plumbi Subacetatis.
L. Potassæ Hydras -	} Potassa Caustica.
Potassa - - -	

FORMER NAME.	PRESENT NAME.
L. Pulvis Ipecacuanhæ Compositus - - -	}
E. ,, ,, ,,	Pulvis Ipecacuanhæ cum Opio.
D. ,, ,, ,,	
L. ,, Kino Compositus	Pulvis Kino cum Opio.
L. Quinæ Disulphas - -	}
E. ,, Sulphas - -	Quiniæ Sulphas.
D. ,, ,, - -	}
L. Sodæ Potassio-Tartras -	Sodæ et Potassæ Tartras.
L. Spiritus Ætheris Nitrici -	}
E. ,, ,, ,, -	Spiritus Ætheris Nitrosi.
D. ,, Æthereus Nitrosus	}
E. ,, Lavandulæ Compositus - -	Tinctura Lavandulæ Composita.
E. Sublimatus Corrosivus -	} Hydrargyrum Corrosivum
D. Sublimatum Corrosivum -	Sublimatum.
E. Syrupus Simplex - -	}
D. ,, ,, - -	Syrupus.
E. Tinctura Buchu - -	}
D. ,, ,, - -	Tinctura Bucco.
L. ,, Camphoræ Composita - -	} Tinctura Camphoræ cum Opio.
E. ,, Camphoræ -	}
D. ,, ,, -	Spiritus Camphoræ.
L. ,, Catechu Composita - -	} Tinctura Catechu.
D. ,, Chirettæ - -	,, Chiratæ.
L. ,, Cinchonæ - -	}
E. ,, ,, - -	,, Cinchonæ Flavæ.
D. ,, Cocci Cacti -	,, Cocci.
L. ,, Colchici - -	
E. ,, ,, - -	}
D. ,, Seminum Colchici - -	,, Colchici Seminis.
L. ,, Ferri Sesquichloridi -	
E. ,, ,, Muriatis	} ,, Ferri Perchloridi.
D. ,, ,, Sesquichloridi	
L. ,, Guaiaci Composita - -	} ,, Guaiaci Ammoniata.
L. ,, Iodinii ,,	} ,, Iodi.
D. ,, ,, ,,	

FORMER NAME.		PRESENT NAME.
D. Tinctura Lupulinæ - -		Tinctura Lupuli.
E. ,, Opii Camphorata	}	,, Camphoræ cum
D. ,, ,, ,,		Opio.
L. ,, Quinæ Compo-	}	,, Quiniæ Composita.
sita - -		
L. ,, Rhei Composita	}	,, Rhei.
D. ,, ,, ,,		
L. ,, Sennæ ,,	}	
E. ,, ,, ,,		,, Sennæ.
D. ,, ,, ,,		
L. ,, Valerianæ ,,	}	,, Valerianæ Ammo-
		niata.
L. Unguentum Antimonii Po-	}	
tassio-Tartratis		Unguentum Antimonii Tar-
E. ,, Antimoniale -	}	tarati.
D. ,, Antimonii		
Tartarizati -		
L. ,, Gallæ Compo-	}	
situm -		,, Gallæ cum Opio.
E. ,, ,, et Opii		
L. ,, Hydrargyri	}	
Ammonio-Chloridi		,, Hydrargyri
E. ,, Hydrargyri		Ammoniati.
Præcipitati Albi		
L. ,, Hydrargyri	}	,, Hydrargyri
Nitrico-Oxidi		Oxidi Rubri.
L. ,, Iodinii Com-	}	
positum -		
E. ,, Iodinei - -		,, Iodi Compo-
D. ,, Iodinii Com-		situm.
positum -		
E. ,, Oxidi Hydrar-	}	,, Hydrargyri
gyri - -		Oxidi Rubri.
E. ,, Plumbi Acetatis	}	,, Plumbi Sub-
D. ,, ,, ,,		acetatis.
L. ,, Zinci - -	}	
E. ,, ,, - -		,, Zinci Oxidi.
D. ,, ,, - -		
L. Vinum Antimonii Potassio-	}	Vinum Antimoniale.
Tartratis -		

NOTES
ON THE BRITISH PHARMACOPŒIA.

PREPARATIONS AND COMPOUNDS.

Acidum Aceticum Dilutum.
This acid is the same strength as that of the Dublin Pharmacopœia, and rather weaker than that of London.

Acidum Aceticum Glaciale.
No process was given in the London Pharmacopœia, and the present one differs from that of Edinburgh or Dublin. It is principally used by photographers.

Acidum Arseniosum.
Commercial arsenious acid purified by sublimation.

Acidum Benzoicum.
Prepared from benzoin by sublimation, following the Dublin directions.

Acidum Citricum.
Lemon juice is directed to be mixed with beer yeast in the proportion of four fluid ounces of yeast to eight pints of juice, and allowed to stand for two days at a temperature between 60° and 70°. When fermentation has ceased, the clear liquor is to be separated from the lees and boiled, and chalk added to it while hot, until there is no more effervescence. The deposit is to be collected and washed with hot distilled water till the liquor passes through colourless. The deposit is then mixed with two pints of distilled water, and four fluid ounces and three-quarters of sulphuric acid, previously diluted with three pints of distilled water, applying sufficient heat to

B

produce ebullition for half-an-hour, constantly stirring; the acid solution to be separated by filtration, and the insoluble matter washed with cold distilled water; the solution and the washings to be mixed and concentrated to the density of 1·21, to be cooled and allowed to stand for twenty-four hours, when the clear liquor is to be poured off from the sulphate of lime which has deposited; the liquor is to be further concentrated until a film forms on its surface, and then to be set aside to cool and crystallize. Some authors recommend the lemon juice to be clarified by heating it with white of egg.

Seventeen grains of citric acid are equal to about half a fluid ounce of fresh lemon juice, and saturate 25 grains of bicarbonate of potash, 20 grains of bicarbonate of soda, 15 grains of carbonate of ammonia.

Acidum Gallicum.

The first of the two forms given by the Dublin College, administered internally, as a styptic, from five grains to twenty. It requires 100 parts of cold water to dissolve it, but is much more soluble in glycerine, requiring only 15 parts of that fluid.

Acidum Hydrochloricum.

The Dublin process; but, by some probable oversight, the application of heat has been omitted in the directions. The Edinburgh College ordered little more than half the quantity of sulphuric acid. This acid, as described in the "Materia Medica," is a trifle stronger than that of the London Pharmacopœia, and the same as that of Edinburgh.

Acidum Hydrochloricum Dilutum.

This acid is slightly stronger than that of either of the last Pharmacopœias, it being in the proportion of three fluid ounces of hydrochloric acid to eight fluid ounces of distilled water; whereas the former ones were in the proportion of three to nine. The difference is so small that it need not affect the dose.

Acidum Hydrocyanicum Dilutum.

This is the London form, containing two per cent. of real acid; it is only half the strength of the Edinburgh. This is a case in point where, as stated in the preface, the Council have chosen the weaker preparation.

Acidum Nitricum.

The Council have in this preparation gone back to the form of the Pharmacopœia of London of 1836, being the same as that of Edinburgh and Dublin, with the omission of the nitrate of silver employed by those Colleges, the specific gravity being 1·5. It is a stronger acid than that of London of 1851, which had a specific gravity of 1·42.

Acidum Nitricum Dilutum.

Two fluid ounces of nitric acid are to be mixed with thirteen fluid ounces of distilled water. This acid is rather stronger than either of the three other Pharmacopœias, of which each differed with the other. Dose—ten to thirty minims, diluted.

Acidum Nitro-Hydrochloricum Dilutum.

Two fluid ounces of nitric acid are to be mixed with twenty-six fluid ounces of distilled water, and then four fluid ounces of hydrochloric acid are to be added. This is an improvement upon the strong acid of the Dublin Pharmacopœia, being much more convenient and manageable. It contains about one minim of strong nitro-hydrochloric acid in five. The dose will be from ten to twenty-five minims, diluted.

Acidum Phosphoricum Dilutum.

The directions for preparing this acid differ slightly from those of the London Pharmacopœia. Care must be taken that the phosphorus is perfectly dissolved before the liquid is transferred to the porcelain capsule; it is rather stronger than the London acid. Dose—ten to thirty minims, diluted.

Acidum Sulphuricum.

A process for purifying sulphuric acid of commerce, which cannot be readily carried out.

Acidum Sulphuricum Aromaticum.

This preparation, like that of Edinburgh and Dublin, contains cinnamon and ginger in addition to the acid and spirit and is rather more than one-fourth weaker than they were Dose—ten to twenty minims, diluted.

Acidum Sulphuricum Dilutum.

This dilute acid does not exactly agree with either of the Colleges. It is made in the proportion of three fluid ounces

of sulphuric acid to thirty-five fluid ounces of distilled water;
it is a little weaker than the London, and very nearly the same
as the Edinburgh and Dublin. Dose—ten to twenty minims,
diluted.

Acidum Sulphurosum.

Introduced for the first time: it forms soluble sulphites
with the alkalies, which salts have not hitherto been considered of much importance.

Acidum Tannicum.

This acid, commonly known as tannin, is to be prepared by
a process the same as given in the Dublin Pharmacopœia; it
is powerfully astringent, and, besides being used in the form
of suppositories and lozenges, as directed in the P. B., it is
frequently given internally in four or five grain doses, and
also as a gargle in the proportion of half a drachm to half a
pint of water; half an ounce may be dissolved in an ounce of
glycerine.

Acidum Tartaricum.

Is to be prepared in a manner similar to that directed in
the London Pharmacopœia of 1836, and in the Edinburgh,
with the exception that chloride of calcium is used in place
of the hydrochloric acid and a portion of the prepared chalk;
it is frequently used in the same way as citric acid for making
effervescing powders or draughts in the proportion of
twenty or thirty grains of acid to twenty-five or thirty-five
of bicarbonate of soda or potash.

Aconitia.

This powerful and poisonous alkaloid, generally known as
aconitine, had a place in the London Pharmacopœia of 1836,
was omitted in 1851, but is now reinserted; the process then
adopted has not been considered a successful one; that now
given differs materially from it. The substance of the process
is as follows:—Aconite root in a coarse powder is to be mixed
with rectified spirit, and heated until ebullition commences,
then allowed to cool and macerate for four days; the whole
is then to be put into the percolator, adding more spirit until
the root is exhausted. The greater portion of the spirit is to
be distilled off, and the remainder evaporated by water-bath
to the state of an extract. This extract is to be thoroughly

mixed with twice its weight of boiling distilled water, and, when cooled to the temperature of the atmosphere, to be filtered through paper. To this filtered liquid, solution of ammonia is to be added in slight excess, and then heated over a water-bath—the precipitate to be separated on a filter and dried: this dry precipitate is to be reduced to coarse powder, and macerated in successive portions of æther with frequent agitation. The several products to be decanted and mixed, and the æther distilled off until the extract is dry. This dry extract is to be dissolved in warm distilled water acidulated with sulphuric acid, and when the solution is cold it is to be precipitated by the cautious addition of solution of ammonia diluted with four times its bulk of distilled water. The precipitate to be washed on a filter with a small quantity of cold distilled water, and dried by slight pressure between folds of filtering paper. A process is given in Royle's "Materia Medica," by Dr. Headland, which he considers a very good one. Its chief employment hitherto has been externally as an ointment, in the proportion of one or two grains to a drachm of lard, in neuralgic affections.

Adeps Præparatus.

The fat of the hog is to be freed as much as possible from the membrane with a knife, then melted in a water-bath at a boiling heat and strained, then heated a second time and stirred continually until it becomes clear, and entirely free from water. The author is still an advocate for washing the fat after the membrane has been removed, with a small quantity of water, before melting and straining.

Æther.

The preparation is carried out in a manner similar to that of the Edinburgh Pharmacopœia. The specific gravity is given as 0·735.

Alumen Exsiccatum.

Alum deprived of its water of crystallization by heat, more commonly known as burnt alum, and used principally in veterinary practice.

Ammoniæ Benzoas.

Now introduced for the first time: a combination of benzoic acid and ammonia, said to be given with benefit in the gouty diathesis. Dose—five to twenty grains, freely soluble in any of the ordinary fluid vehicles.

Ammoniæ Phosphas.

For the first time in Pharmacopœia. The process is a simple combination of solutions of phosphoric acid and ammonia evaporated and crystallized; it is given in gout and rheumatism. Dose—ten to thirty grains.

Antimonii Oxidum.

Prepared by precipitation from the solution of terchloride of antimony by water and carbonate of soda, washing the precipitate with distilled water and drying at a temperature not exceeding 212°.

Antimonium Sulphuratum.

In this preparation the London process has been adopted.

Antimonium Tartaratum.

The process now given is that of the Dublin Pharmacopœia.

Aqua Anethi.

Prepared by distillation from the fruit (seeds).

Aqua Camphoræ.

Formerly mistura camphoræ, prepared by the simple immersion and maceration of camphor in water, the spirit of the London and Dublin Colleges and the sugar and almonds of the Edinburgh being dispensed with.

Aqua Carui.

By distillation from the fruit (seeds), the essence of the Dublin College being rejected.

Aqua Cinnamomi.

By distillation from the bark and not from the essence.

Aqua Destillata.

Water freed from impurities by distillation, rejecting the first three or four pints.

Aqua Fœniculi.
As aqua anethi.

Aqua Laurocerasi.
The process is that of the Dublin College, the compound spirit of lavender of the Edinburgh being omitted. An uncertain preparation. The late Dr. Pereira gave the dose from thirty to sixty minims; but, from the uncertainty attached to it, it is more frequently given in doses of ten minims.

Aqua Menthæ Piperitæ.
Now prepared with the oil by distillation, one-fourth less oil being ordered than when prepared by trituration and filtration, the herb of the London and Edinburgh Colleges and the essence of the Dublin being alike put aside.

Aqua Menthæ Viridis.
As aqua menthæ piperitæ.

Aqua Pimentæ.
By distillation with the berries, rather less than one ounce more to the gallon being used than last, and the spirit of the Edinburgh being left out, the Dublin essence as before being discontinued.

Aqua Rosæ.
With the fresh petals, by distillation, and without any addition of spirit. Some practical men consider the water distilled from pickled petals as good or better, with the advantage of being able to distil at any season of the year, avoiding the probability of the water becoming sour from long keeping, and also by the pickling process diminishing the chance of running short in a year of scarcity, not an improbable occurrence.

Aqua Sambuci.
From the fresh flowers. The former remarks apply equally well in this case.

Argenti Nitras.
Identical with former processes.

Argenti Oxidum.

This is the Dublin preparation. Prescribers should bear in mind that it is incompatible with conserve and most of the essential oils and creosote, as combustion takes place, either immediately upon mixing or subsequently.

Atropia.

This active alkaloid now takes the place of the sulphate of the London College: it is employed chiefly by the oculist in the place of extract of belladonna, being a cleaner and perhaps more certain agent.

Beberiæ Sulphas.

Introduced for the first time in the Pharmacopœia. It is tonic and antiperiodic, and given in doses of three to ten grains, and to the amount of a scruple or more between the paroxysms in intermittents.

Bismuthum Album.

The directions for this preparation are those of the Dublin Pharmacopœia as given for bismuthi subnitras, similar to those of London and Edinburgh for the bismuthi nitras of the former, and bismuthum album of the latter. It is to be regretted that the bismuthi carbonas was not now introduced into the P. B., being more compatible with the carbonates of the alkalies, with which it is often prescribed.

Calcis Carbonas Præcipitata.

Prepared according to the Dublin Pharmacopœia by mixing hot solutions of chloride of calcium and carbonate of soda, in the proportion of five ounces of chloride of calcium and thirteen ounces of carbonate of soda, each dissolved in two pints of boiling distilled water, washing and drying the precipitate. It is prepared largely as an article of commerce, and the great consumption is in the preparation of tooth powders.

Calcis Hydras.

Slaked lime, used in the preparation of lime water.

Calcis Phosphas Præcipitata.

Prepared according to the Dublin form, given internally in doses of five to twenty grains.

Calomelas.

In this case, the Council have given up the name of hydrargyri chloridum of the London Pharmacopœias of 1836 and 1851, and have adopted that of Edinburgh and Dublin. It is prepared by a process similar to that of the Dublin Pharmacopœia, with but slight variation in the detail.

Carbo Animalis Purificatus.

Prepared from bone black, as Edinburgh and Dublin, instead of bullocks' blood, as in London " Materia Medica;" chiefly used for decolourizing.

Cataplasma Carbonis.

The London form, with a very slight deviation in weight, in consequence of the avoirdupois ounce taking the place of the troy.

Cataplasma Conii.

In this poultice one ounce of hemlock leaf is substituted for one ounce of extract, with three ounces of linseed meal in place of four and a half, or a sufficiency. This and all the other forms for poultices are from the London Pharmacopœia, as neither the Edinburgh nor Dublin gave any forms.

Cataplasma Fermenti.

No change.

Cataplasma Lini.

The addition of olive oil, in the proportion of half a fluid ounce to four ounces of linseed meal, and ten fluid ounces of boiling water, is now ordered.

Cataplasma Sinapis.

Equal parts of linseed meal and mustard as before, with ten ounces of boiling water. In the last the quantity of water was to be made into a poultice, with as much of the mixed powders as was necessary.

Cataplasma Sodæ Chloratæ.

The quantity of linseed meal is reduced from four ounces and a half troy to four ounces avoirdupois, the quantity of solution of chlorinated soda, namely, two ounces, being the

same, and the water increased from six to eight ounces.
These appear small alterations, but they are nevertheless
useful in determining the quantity of water required.

Chloroformum.

The process now given differs slightly in the detail from
that of London or Dublin. It is prepared by distilling rectified spirit with chlorinated lime, and is made in quantity
almost exclusively by manufacturing chemists. It enters into
the composition of the spirit of chloroform of the P. B. and
the long-used popular preparation known as chloric æther.
Care should be taken not to confound the former with the
latter, as the first contains only one fluid part of chloroform
in twenty; whereas the second has one in eight, as usually
made. The power of chloroform as a solvent and anæsthetic
is well known; a work of considerable size might be written
upon the various applications of it; but that is not within the
intention of the present volume.

Collodium.

The pyroxylin as prepared according to the form given in
Appendix A of the P. B., is not suitable for the purpose of
making collodium, the nitric acid used in the process being
too strong: the pyroxylin so made is not sufficiently soluble.
Muspratt gives the following process for preparing pyroxylin
suitable for making photographic collodium, which would be
equally applicable for surgical purposes:—Mix together in
a large and perfectly dry basin equal parts of commercial oil
of vitriol, and nitric acid specific gravity 1·42. The temperature
of the mixed acids rises to about 150°, and it must be maintained at that temperature; immerse in the mixture in small
quantities at a time, pulled out into flat pieces, as much of
the best cotton wool as the liquid will conveniently cover,
stirring it about with two thick glass rods for the space of
five minutes; it is now to be thoroughly washed with water,
and lastly, a little carbonate of soda to be added to the water,
to remove all traces of acidity. It is to be soaked for an
hour or two in water, and then taken out, squeezed, and
hung up in a safe place to dry spontaneously, pulling it out
when nearly dry into small tufts, so as to dry perfectly. The
proper strength of the nitric acid is to be particularly attended
to. For preparing the collodium, mix together one part by
ᵐeasure of absolute æther ·725, and three parts by measure of

absolute alcohol ·800, and to every fluid ounce of this mixture add from six to eight grains of the pyroxylin. Shake the mixture for some minutes, and then set it aside undisturbed for several days, at the end of which time the clear solution may be drawn off. (Muspratt's Chemistry.) The addition of ten grains of palm oil, or ten minims of castor oil, to each ounce of collodium, renders it more elastic and less liable to crack when used surgically.

Confectio Piperis.

In compounding this apparently simple preparation, the Council have followed neither of the former forms, either in material or proportion; it is now a mixture of black pepper, caraway and honey, in the proportion of one part of pepper in ten: the London and Edinburgh form had one part in nine of pepper, the Dublin one in eight. The elecampane, fennel and sugar of London, the liquorice, fennel, and sugar of Edinburgh, and the liquorice, sugar and oil of fennel of Dublin are omitted, so that the preparation differs with that of each of the Colleges.

Confectio Rosæ Caninæ.

Here again there is a change of proportions. The present gives one part of hips to two of sugar, the London twelve parts to twenty, the Edinburgh one to three.

Confectio Rosæ Gallicæ.

The London and Edinburgh Colleges have been followed, and but a very slight difference existed between them and the Dublin in proportion, and that not important.

Confectio Scammonii.

The form of the Dublin College has been retained, the proportion of scammony being as nearly as possible the same as that of the London.

Confectio Sennæ.

This confection closely resembles that of the London and the electuary of the Edinburgh College. There are several minor alterations, but which do not affect the flavour, strength, or appearance; it differs with that of the Dublin in flavour, as the oil of caraway of that College is omitted, and white sugar is used in place of their brown.

Confectio Sulphuris.

The original of this was that of Dublin, but it has suffered some pruning. The quantity of sulphur, 4 oz., remains the same; the bitartrate of potash, commonly known as cream of tartar, now called acid tartrate of potash, being reduced one half, namely, from two ounces to one ; the clarified honey, syrup of ginger, and syrup of saffron being omitted, syrup of orange taking the place of them.

Confectio Terebinthinæ.

A mixture of oil of turpentine one fluid ounce, liquorice powder one ounce, and two ounces of clarified honey, as Dublin Pharmacopœia.

Creta Præparata.

Prepared by elutriation, according to the last Dublin or London of 1836.

Cupri Sulphas.

The commercial sulphate purified by solution in boiling distilled water, filtration, and crystallization.

Decoctum Aloes Compositum.

The alterations made in this preparation are of an important character : it has rather more than two-thirds the quantity of aloes, myrrh and saffron, that the London had, with the same proportion of liquorice and compound tincture of cardamoms, and a little more carbonate of potash ; it has half as much more aloes as the Edinburgh, leaving the liquorice and other ingredients the same ; it has the same proportions as the Dublin, but the directions for preparing it are more distinct and definite. The P. B. directs the ingredients to be boiled in fourteen ounces of water for ten minutes in a covered vessel, and when cold to strain and add the tincture with as much water as will make the quantity up to sixteen fluid ounces ; whereas the Dublin ordered the ingredients to be boiled for ten minutes in a covered vessel, and, after cooling and straining, to add as much of the tincture as would make sixteen fluid ounces. The necessity of keeping two preparations, on the part of the London and Edinburgh dispenser, becomes apparent, as no one accustomed to the use of the old preparations will like the flavour of the new, to say nothing of the increased aperient qualities. The definite quantity of the tincture in the present form is an improvement upon the indefinite quantity of the Dublin, as experience proves that a ten minutes' boiling will not always realize the same product.

Decoctum Cetrariæ.

The proportion of the Dublin Pharmacopœia has been adopted in this decoction, being one ounce of moss to the pint in place of five drachms of London.

Decoctum Cinchonæ Flavæ.

The decoction of the yellow bark only is now seemingly recognized, the quantity of bark to sixteen ounces of product being one ounce, rather more than a fifth less than London, the same as Edinburgh, excepting the difference being avoirdupois and troy weight, and agreeing with Dublin : the product when finished is now made to measure sixteen ounces, an improvement upon the former uncertain quantity of the London Pharmacopœia.

Decoctum Granati Radicis.

The same as that of the London College, excepting the change of weights.

Decoctum Hæmatoxyli.

In this case the Edinburgh College has been ostensibly followed in the addition of cinnamon to the logwood, but then deviated therefrom by making the product measure sixteen ounces in place of ten. Neither the London nor Dublin Colleges employed the cinnamon, and the Dublin had double the quantity of logwood. The present has one ounce of log-wood and sixty grains of cinnamon to make sixteen ounces.

Decoctum Hordei.

The proportions differ with both the London and Dublin, but in so simple a matter it cannot be of any moment ; the compound decoction of London and the mixture of Edinburgh, similar preparations, containing figs, raisins and liquorice, in addition to the barley, have been omitted.

Decoctum Papaveris.

The changes in this are too small to require being pointed

out. A solution made by dissolving a given quantity of extract in boiling water would perhaps have answered as well, and been more convenient.

Decoctum Pareiræ.

The London process, with a slight increase of sixty grains in the strength, caused probably by the adoption of the avoirdupois ounce, and having no actual division of the ounce representing an eighth, sixth, or third, one ounce and a half avoirdupois being substituted for ten drachms.

Decoctum Quercus.

The Dublin College is followed in this case, the Council departing from their general good plan, of making the product measure a given quantity.

Decoctum Sarsæ.

The same as the London and Edinburgh forms, bearing in mind the difference between avoirdupois and troy weight. Rather stronger than the Dublin.

Decoctum Sarsæ Compositum.

There are several minor alterations of quantity in the sassafras, guaiac (formerly known as guaiacum), liquorice and mezereon, not important in themselves. The sarsaparilla is ordered not to be split; it should be cut into small pieces.

Decoctum Scoparii.

A simple decoction of broom tops, in the proportion of half an ounce in the eight ounces, according to the Dublin directions, the juniper berries, and taraxacum root of London, and the juniper tops and bitartrate of potash of Edinburgh being left out.

Decoctum Taraxaci.

The dried root, in the proportion of an ounce in a pint, is now ordered, the substitution of the dried for the fresh root being an improvement, inasmuch as to use the fresh implies collecting it at any season when required; but for the dry it may be collected at the best time and opportunity, and can be preserved in the dry state for an almost indefinite period.

Digitalinum.

This very powerful alkaloid is introduced for the first time ; its employment requires the greatest possible caution, the dose being $\frac{1}{30}$ to $\frac{1}{16}$ of a grain. The process resembles that given in " Parrish's Practical Pharmacy."

Elaterium.

The process is essentially the same as that formerly given for extract of elaterium.

Emplastrum Ammoniaci cum Hydrargyro.

The form of the London and Edinburgh Colleges has been followed, but the fact of the ammoniac requiring to be strained as well as liquefied has apparently been overlooked; the resin, turpentine, and litharge plaster of Dublin being left out.

Emplastrum Belladonnæ.

The proportion of extract and plaster is the same as that of London, namely, equal, but employing half soap and half resin plasters instead of all soap, thereby giving more adhesiveness ; it contains twice the quantity of extract of the Edinburgh and Dublin forms, in which one part of extract and two of resin plaster were used. Would not a plaster made with the alkaloid atropia be equally efficacious and less unpleasant, being free from odour and colour ?

Emplastrum Calefaciens.

This is a compromise between the emplastrum calefaciens of Dublin and the emplastrum cantharidis compositum of Edinburgh ; by the addition of a watery infusion of cantharides, it is made more stimulating as a warm plaster than the emplastrum picis.

Emplastrum Cantharidis.

The form of the London College in its entirety is retained, differing from the Edinburgh by the employment of a portion of lard and less resin, and having one-third more cantharides ; differing with the Dublin by the use of some suet, and consequently less wax, resin and lard, the quantity of cantharides being the same.

Emplastrum Ferri.

This is the plaster of the Dublin College sometimes known as emplastrum thuris, or strengthening plaster. It contains but half the quantity of iron that the Edinburgh form did, and employs Burgundy pitch in place of resin, oil and wax.

Emplastrum Galbani.

In this case the Edinburgh form has been adhered to : it contains but half the quantity of galbanum, of the London, ammoniac and yellow wax taking the place of turpentine and gum thus, or frankincense.

Emplastrum Hydrargyri.

This is the Edinburgh form: it contains one-third more mercury than the London, omitting the small quantity of sulphur ordered by that College, adding one ounce of resin and one ounce of oil to six ounces of litharge plaster; identical in proportion of mercury with the Dublin, but omitting the oil of turpentine.

Emplastrum Lithargyri.

This approximates closely to the Edinburgh and Dublin Colleges, containing rather less litharge than the London.

Emplastrum Opii.

This plaster is prepared in accordance with that of the Dublin College, being a simple combination of powdered opium and resin plaster in the proportion of one part of opium to nine of plaster.

Emplastrum Picis.

This is the plaster of the London College : the great difference between it and the Edinburgh is that the latter contains no frankincense, which forms one-fourth of the P. B. and P. L. plaster.

Emplastrum Resinæ.

The Council, in this instance, have followed the Dublin College, which is perhaps to be regretted, as the addition of the soap to the resin and litharge plaster renders it too much like the soap plaster, and thus in some measure does away with the distinctive resinous or adhesive quality of that of the London and Edinburgh Colleges.

Emplastrum Saponis.

This is the London College form, avoiding the strongly smelling gum plaster of Edinburgh, and containing one third more soap than the Dublin plaster. In preparing the plasters the Council have wisely selected apparently the best form of the three Colleges, and adhered to it. It would have been a cause of rejoicing if the same plan could have been adopted in all the compound preparations, as many seemingly trivial alterations might then have been avoided.

Enema Aloes.

The form is that of London: substituting mucilage of starch for decoction of barley. Neither of the other Colleges used this preparation.

Enema Assafœtidæ.

This enema is made with six fluid drachms of tincture of assafœtida, and six ounces of mucilage of starch, being different to either of the former preparations. The London form was sixty grains of gum assafœtida to half a pint of decoction of barley; the Edinburgh was two fluid drachms of tincture of assafœtida in about sixteen ounces of cathartic enema; the Dublin was two fluid drachms of tincture of assafœtida with twelve ounces of warm water.

Enema Magnesiæ Sulphatis.

This enema, composed of one ounce of sulphate of magnesia, and one fluid ounce of olive oil, with fifteen fluid ounces of mucilage of starch, is the same as that of Dublin, with the exception of employing fifteen ounces of mucilage of starch, instead of sixteen ounces of decoction of barley. There was no corresponding enema in the London Pharmacopœia nearer than the enema of extract of colocynth, soft soap and water, which is now omitted. The cathartic enema of Edinburgh contained senna and sugar in addition to the sulphate of magnesia and oil, using water as the vehicle.

Enema Opii.

Half a fluid drachm of tincture of opium, with two ounces of mucilage of starch; containing twice the quantity of tincture that the London had, and the same as Edinburgh.

c

Enema Tabaci.

Twenty grains of tobacco leaf infused in eight fluid ounces of boiling water for half-an-hour. London had twenty grains and ten ounces of water infused for an hour; Edinburgh, from fifteen to thirty grains, infused for half-an-hour in eight ounces of water; and Dublin had twenty grains infused for an hour with eight ounces of water.

Enema Terebinthinæ.

One fluid ounce of oil of turpentine with fifteen fluid ounces of mucilage of starch. London and Edinburgh used yolk of egg to suspend the oil, the former with decoction of barley, the latter water; the Dublin, mucilage of barley only.

Extractum Aconiti.

The pharmaceutical chemist, and every one undertaking to prepare the fresh vegetable extracts, should pay particular attention to the directions given, as they differ materially with all former ones. The fresh leaves and flowering tops are to be bruised, and the juice expressed therefrom is to be heated gradually to 130°, and then the colouring matter is to be separated by means of a calico filter or strainer. (The colouring matter should be put aside in a cool place.) The strained liquor is to be heated to 200°, to separate the albumen (which is to be rejected), and again filtered or strained. The filtrate or strained liquor is to be evaporated by a water bath heat to the consistence of a thin syrup, when the colouring matter or chlorophyll, previously separated, is to be added, and the whole assiduously stirred, continuing the evaporation at a temperature not exceeding 140°, until the extract is of a proper consistence.

Extractum Aloes Barbadensis.

Boiling distilled water, in the proportion of one gallon to one pound of aloes broken into small fragments, is to be poured upon the aloes and stirred until thoroughly mixed, and after being left for twelve hours at rest, the clear liquid is to be poured off, and the remainder strained; the mixed liquors to be evaporated to a proper consistence by a water bath or current of warm air. By the London directions maceration with gentle heat was employed for three days, and after allowing the dregs to subside, the strained liquor was evaporated.

Extractum Aloes Socotrinæ.

Prepared as extractum aloes barbadensis. The Dublin Pharmacopœia directed hepatic aloes to be boiled in water until dissolved, when cold, the dregs having subsided, the clear liquid to be poured off, and evaporated to a proper consistence.

Extractum Anthemidis.

Prepared by digesting chamomile flowers in water, and pressing twice, and at the end of the process adding fifteen minims of oil of chamomile for every pound of flowers used.

Extractum Belæ Liquidum.

Now in the Pharmacopœia for the first time: prepared by macerating one pound of bael for twelve hours, in four pints of cold distilled water; the clear liquor being poured off, it is to be macerated twice more for one hour, each time in four pints of water, the marc pressed, the mixed liquors filtered through flannel, and evaporated to fourteen ounces, when two ounces of spirit are to be added. One fluid ounce represents one ounce of bael. Dose—two or three fluid drachms.

Extractum Belladonnæ.
Extractum Conii.
Extractum Hyoscyami.

These three extracts are to be prepared in the same manner as the aconite, bearing in mind that the young tender branches are to be used as well as the leaves. To filter through calico scarcely conveys a correct impression of the work to be done; we generally strain through calico, flannel bags and hair sieves, and filter through paper.

Extractum Calumbæ.

This is a new introduction, and the process an imperfect one: the quantity of proof spirit is insufficient to exhaust the calumbo. The ordinary directions for percolating are neglected; and, therefore, the result, as might be expected, is unsatisfactory. After packing in the percolator the spirit should be displaced in the usual way; and then, after recovering the spirit by distillation, the residue should be evaporated by water or steam bath to a proper consistence.

Extractum Cannabis Indicæ.

An alcoholic extract new to the Pharmacopœia: prepared by distilling the spirit from a tincture, and evaporating the residue. Pereira states the dose as one grain to five; but much smaller doses are given to commence with.

Extractum Cinchonæ Flavæ Liquidum.

The infusum cinchonæ spissatum of London: percolation is used instead of maceration for exhausting the bark; in other respects, the process is substantially the same.

Extractum Colchici.

This differs entirely with the London process, which ordered the undefecated juice to be at once evaporated to a proper consistence; the feculence is now to be allowed to subside, and the clear liquor to be heated to 212°, strained through flannel, and evaporated by a water bath, at a temperature not exceeding 160°.

Extractum Colchici Aceticum.

Similar process to the preceding, with the addition of six fluid ounces of acetic acid to seven pounds of corms, being one fluid ounce of acid to nineteen ounces by weight, of corms. The London had one fluid ounce of acid to four ounces of corms, the Edinburgh the same proportions, and the Dublin one to four of the dried corms.

Extractum Colocynthidis Compositum.

This extract is that of London 1836 restored: it differs from the pilula colocynthidis composita of 1851, by having the colocynth exhausted with proof spirit, in place of water, and using hard soap instead of soft, and giving the maker the option of using either the resin of scammony, or the gum-resin, known as virgin scammony.

Extractum Ergotæ Liquidum.

One of the new preparations: ergot in coarse powder is to be put into a percolator, and washed æther to be passed through it to free it from its oil. The marc is then to be removed from the percolator, and digested for twelve hours with distilled water, at a temperature of 160°, then pressed, strained, and evaporated; and to nine fluid ounces of liquor so prepared from one pound of ergot, eight ounces of rectified spirit are to be added, and at the expiration of an hour filtered, the product measuring sixteen fluid ounces. Each fluid ounce so prepared being equivalent to one ounce, by weight, of ergot, the dose would be from twenty to sixty minims. No provision is made for removing the whole of the æther before adding the water in which it is to be digested. Would it not have been better to have driven out all the æther by water, and then having made up the quantity of water, digested the marc for twelve hours at 160°, as directed? The rationale of the process is based upon the assumption that the activity of ergot depends upon the aqueous extract, and not the oil.

Extractum Filicis Liquidum.

New preparation in Pharmacopœia. The fern root in coarse powder, packed in a percolator, is to be exhausted with æther; the æther to be evaporated in a water-bath, or recovered by distillation, preserving the liquid oily extract. The successful operator, with care, will recover the greater portion of the æther, which may be reserved for a future operation; this liquid extract, commonly known as oil of male fern, is employed in expelling tape worm: the plan usually adopted is to starve the patient, as regards solid food, after a substantial early dinner, till the following morning, when, to an adult, one fluid drachm of the fluid extract should be given, rubbed up with the yolk of an egg, or half an ounce of mucilage of gum, adding sufficient water to make an ordinary twelve drachm draught. An hour after this draught, one ounce of castor oil should be administered, and immediately after its operation, a basin of good strong beef-tea or soup—the oil or liquid extract being good, and the worm present, the result is very generally successful.

Extractum Gentianæ.

The root is to be macerated in water for two hours, then boiled for fifteen minutes, pressed, strained, and evaporated by a water-bath. The London and Dublin ordered maceration and expression without heat, the Edinburgh percolation with temperate distilled water. The present process, however good, would scarcely be followed by a manufacturer who wished to obtain the largest product: he would macerate with more than one quantity of water.

Extractum Glycyrrhizæ.

The root is to be dried, coarsely powdered, then macerated
for twelve hours with cold distilled water, and exhausted by
percolation, heated to 212°, strained, and evaporated to a
proper consistence. The London ordered maceration with
hot water, decoction, and evaporation; the Edinburgh, percolation with temperate distilled water; Dublin, maceration
with cold water, expression, and evaporation. Commercially
speaking, the above process would scarcely be followed.

Extractum Hæmatoxyli.

By maceration with boiling distilled water, decoction and
evaporation, as London and Edinburgh.

Extractum Jalapæ.

The jalap is to be macerated for seven days with rectified
spirit, then pressed and filtered, and the spirit recovered by
distillation, leaving a soft extract; the residual jalap to be
macerated in water for four hours, then pressed, strained
through flannel, and evaporated to a soft extract; the two
extracts to be mixed, and brought to a proper consistence at
a temperature not exceeding 140°. The London ordered only
four days' maceration with the spirit; in other respects, the
directions were virtually the same. The Edinburgh extract
was a resin, and prepared by displacement with rectified
spirit, recovering as much of the spirit as practicable, by distillation, and evaporating the residue to a proper consistence.

Extractum Krameriæ.

The rhatany, in coarse powder, is to be exhausted with cold
distilled water, by percolation, and the liquor evaporated by
a water-bath to a proper consistence: astringent and tonic.
In doses from five to twenty grains.

Extractum Lupuli.

The hop is to be macerated with rectified spirit for seven
days, the tincture pressed out and filtered, and the spirit
distilled off, leaving a soft extract; the residual hop is then
to be boiled for one hour with water, the liquor expressed,
strained, and evaporated, to the consistence of a soft extract;
the two extracted portions are then to be mixed and reduced
by evaporation, at a temperature not exceeding 140°, to a

proper consistence. The difference between this process and that of London and Edinburgh, consists in the employment of the spirit in the first part of the operation.

Extractum Nucis Vomicæ.

There is little or no difference between the process now given, and that of London or Edinburgh, excepting that the Edinburgh gave the option of exhausting the coarsely powdered nux vomica, either by percolation or repeated boilings with rectified spirit. But now, the coarsely powdered nux vomica is to be exhausted by repeated boilings with rectified spirit, then strained, the spirit distilled off, and the residue evaporated to the state of an extract. Dose—¼ grain to two or three grains, gradually increased.—Pereira.

Extractum Opii.

Prepared by maceration in repeated quantities of cold distilled water, expressing strongly each time, and evaporating the strained liquors to a proper consistence.

Extractum Opii Liquidum.

Introduced for the first time into the Pharmacopœia: consists of one ounce of extract of opium, dissolved in seventeen fluid ounces of distilled water, and three of rectified spirit, so as to make one pint. The dose is about the same as that of tincture of opium.

Extráctum Pareiræ Liquidum.

This preparation is new to the Pharmacopœia: the pareira in coarse powder is to be macerated in boiling distilled water for twenty-four hours, then exhausted by percolation with boiling distilled water; the clear liquor obtained from one pound of pareira is to be evaporated to thirteen fluid ounces, and, when cold, three fluid ounces of rectified spirit are to be added, and the whole filtered. Dose—one to two fluid drachms.

The pareira is very hard to powder: when bruised, it can be exhausted quite as effectually by digestion in boiling water as by percolation.

Extractum Quassiæ.

The quassia is to be macerated with cold distilled water for twelve hours, then packed in a percolator, and exhausted

by passing through it a sufficient quantity of cold distilled
water. The liquid evaporated, and before it has become too
thick, it is to be filtered, and then evaporated to a proper
consistence. Dose—two to five grains.

Extractum Rhei.

The London process, with ten fluid ounces of rectified
spirit, and five pints of distilled water, to one pound of
rhubarb; the spirit used is not ordered to be distilled off,
but, after straining, to be evaporated away with the water at
a temperature not exceeding 160°. The Edinburgh and
Dublin Colleges used water only for exhausting the rhubarb.

Extractum Sarsæ Liquidum.

. Similar to the London, with the exception that the sarsaparilla is not to be boiled, but macerated twice in distilled
water at 160°, then expressed and filtered, and the mixed
liquors evaporated by a water-bath, until reduced to seven
fluid ounces, as the product from one pound of sarsaparilla;
the specific gravity being 1·13. When cold, one ounce of
spirit is to be added. The Edinburgh and Dublin forms
contained less sarsaparilla, and the Edinburgh ordered the
sarsaparilla, after digesting in the water for two hours, to be
taken out and bruised—a part of the process now well omitted.
One fluid ounce of the present preparation represents two
ounces of sarsaparilla. The specific gravity should be about
1·095.

Extractum Stramonii.

The seeds in coarse powder are to be exhausted by percolation with proof spirit, as in the Edinburgh form; the
spirit distilled off, and the residue evaporated by a water-bath.

Extractum Taraxaci.

The process now given is entirely different to that employed before: the fresh root is to be thoroughly bruised or
crushed, and the expressed juice allowed to deposit (say from
evening to the following morning in a cold dry place), the
clear liquor to be brought up to a temperature of 212°, and
maintained thereat for ten minutes; to be then strained and
evaporated by a water-bath at a temperature not exceeding
160', to a proper consistence. The root should be operated
upon as soon after collecting as convenient. The quality of
the product, if the process be strictly followed, will be good.

Fel Bovinum Purificatum.

New to the Pharmacopœia. Fresh ox bile is to be agitated with rectified spirit, in the proportion of one pint of bile to two of spirit, and set aside for twelve hours, until the sediment has subsided. The clear solution is then to be evaporated in a porcelain capsule, on a water-bath, until it acquires the consistence of a vegetable extract. Dose—from five to twenty grains, in pills.

Ferri Arsenias.

A new preparation. In cancer, psoriasis, &c., it has been given in doses of $\frac{1}{16}$ to $\frac{1}{12}$ of a grain, usually combined with phosphate of iron; externally used in ointments containing about 30 grains to the ounce.—" Parrish's Practical Pharmacy."

Ferri Carbonas Saccharata.

The directions of the Dublin College have been followed: the dry sugar is now to be mixed with the carbonate of iron, recently prepared, and subjected to pressure. The sugar was before ordered to be dissolved in a portion of the water before being mixed with the carbonate.

Ferri et Ammoniæ Citras.

The London form has been rejected for the present one based upon that of Dublin. A solution of persulphate of iron is first made. (Vide Appendix, A : P.B.)

From this the hydrated peroxide of iron is to be precipitated by ammonia, washed and added to the citric acid previously dissolved in distilled water; the solution to be made neutral by the addition of ammonia, then evaporated and scaled. The quantity of iron appears insufficient to produce a good scaling preparation.

Ferri et Quiniæ Citras.

Introduced for the first time into the Pharmacopœia, though for a long time prescribed with advantage. Dose—from three to ten grains.

Ferri Iodidum.

The iron, iodine and water are to be heated gently for about ten minutes. The heat to be then raised, and the

solution boiled until it loses its red colour. The filtered
solution to be evaporated down in a polished iron dish until
a drop taken out on the point of an iron wire solidifies on
cooling, the liquid then to be poured upon a porcelain dish,
and as soon as solidified to be broken into fragments, and
kept in well-stoppered bottles. The Edinburgh ordered the
solution to be evaporated in a basin shut up in a small
convenient space not communicating with the general atmosphere; the Dublin to evaporate the solution in a flask, and,
if necessary, break it to remove the iodide.

Ferri Oxidum Magneticum.

The Dublin form, using solution of soda in place of solution
of potash or ammonia. Dose—from five to twenty grains.

Ferri Peroxidum.

The hydrated peroxide of iron, of Dublin, is to be heated
in an oven until dry to the touch, then exposed to a heat of
212°, until it ceases to lose weight, then reduced to fine
powder, and preserved in a bottle. This represents the ferri
sesquioxydum of London, and the ferri oxidum rubrum of
Edinburgh; the carbonate of soda and sulphate of iron
process being set aside.

Ferri Peroxydum Hydratum.

Taken from the Dublin Pharmacopœia: four fluid ounces
of the solution of persulphate of iron (vide Appendix A: P. B.)
are to be diluted with a pint of distilled water, and gradually
poured into thirty-three fluid ounces of solution of soda, or a
sufficiency, stirring well for a few minutes; the precipitate to
be collected on a calico strainer, and washed with distilled
water until it ceases to give a precipitate, with chloride of
barium; keep it in a porcelain jar, without drying, with a
ground cover, making the lid air tight by a luting of lard.

Ferri Phosphas.

Three ounces of sulphate of iron are to be dissolved in
two pints of boiling distilled water, and two ounces and a
half of phosphate of soda, with one ounce of acetate of soda
together, in two pints of boiling distilled water; the two
solutions mixed, and after careful stirring, the precipitate to
be washed with hot distilled water on a calico strainer, until
it ceases to give a precipitate with chloride of barium, to be

dried on porous bricks in a stove, at a temperature not exceeding 100°. Dose—from five to twenty grains.

Ferri Sulphas.

Prepared according to the Dublin Pharmacopœia, with iron wire, sulphuric acid, and distilled water. The London and Edinburgh dissolved commercial sulphate in distilled water, acidulated with sulphuric acid, filtered and set aside to crystallize ; London also employing one ounce of iron wire to forty-eight ounces of sulphate.

Ferri Sulphas Exsiccata.

Sulphate of iron exposed to heat until the water is all driven off, and it is converted into a dry greyish white mass, which is to be reduced to powder, as Edinburgh and Dublin.

Ferri Sulphas Granulata.

This also is a Dublin form, and a very convenient preparation for dispensing purposes. Pour a pint and a half of distilled water upon four ounces of iron wire in a porcelain capsule, add four fluid ounces of oil of vitriol, and when the disengagement of gas has nearly ceased, boil for ten minutes. Filter now through paper into a vessel containing eight ounces of rectified spirit, and stir the mixture as it cools, in order that the salt may be obtained in minute granular crystals. Let these, deprived by decantation and draining of the adhering liquid, be washed on a funnel or small percolator with two ounces more spirit ; and when rendered quite dry by repeated pressure between folds of filtering paper, and subsequent exposure for twenty-four hours, beneath a glass bell, over a common dinner plate half filled with oil of vitriol, let them be preserved in a well-stoppered bottle.—Dublin Pharmacopœia.

Ferrum Redactum.

This is the Dublin process for making pulvis ferri or Quevenne's iron, substituting chloride of calcium in the place of caustic potash, in the desiccating tube. Dose—one to six grains.

Ferrum Tartaratum.

Also prepared after the Dublin form : only substituting solution of soda for solution of potash, to precipitate the

hydrated peroxide of iron, and after it has been added to the
acid tartrate of potash : the heat employed is not to exceed
140°.   London used liquor ammoniæ, and Edinburgh carbonate of ammonia, in place of potash or soda.

Hydrargyri Iodidum Rubrum.

The Dublin preparation : made by dissolving one ounce of
corrosive sublimate in twenty-five ounces of distilled water,
and the iodide of potassium in five ounces, and mixing the
cold solutions ; when the precipitate has subsided, pour off
the supernatant liquor, and having put the precipitate upon a
paper filter, wash it with ten ounces of distilled water, and,
lastly, dry it at a temperature not exceeding 212°.

Hydrargyri Iodidum Viride.

The same as London and Dublin.

Hydrargyri Oxidum Rubrum.

Edinburgh process : the difference between it and London
and Dublin being, that these two ordered the whole of the
mercury to be digested with the diluted nitric acid—before
evaporating and drying—whilst the former ordered half the
mercury to be dissolved in the acid, with the aid of a
moderate heat, continuing the heat till a dry salt was formed;
the remainder of the mercury to be triturated with the salt
until a fine uniform powder was obtained, this powder to be
heated in a porcelain vessel, and constantly stirred, till the
acid fumes ceased to be discharged.

Hydrargyrum.

Mercury of commerce distilled, and afterwards boiled for
a few minutes with a little dilute hydrochloric acid, and then
well washed with distilled water and dried.

Hydrargyrum Ammoniatum.

There is no alteration in this preparation except in the
name.   (Vide change of nomenclature).

Hydrargyrum Corrosivum Sublimatum.

Process same as London and Dublin, with the addition of
small portion of black oxide of manganese, to the sulphate

of mercury and chloride of sodium, previous to sublimation. Edinburgh employed some nitric acid with the sulphuric in preparing the sulphate of mercury.

Hydrargyrum cum Cretâ.

The Dublin proportions are now used : namely, one ounce of mercury to two of chalk; London and Edinburgh had three of mercury to five of prepared chalk. Hopes were entertained that something more definite than this uncertain mechanical mixture would be found; it is by no means an uncommon occurrence for the mercury to be rubbed out when working up a stiff pill mass with which it is intended to be combined.

Infusum Anthemidis.

This simple infusion differs with all the last, as they did with each other. To show how the spirit of change reigned, the proportions are placed below :—

P. B.—Chamomile half an ounce, water ten ounces. Infuse for fifteen minutes.

P. L.—Chamomile five drachms, water one pint. Infuse ten minutes.

P. E.—Chamomile, five drachms, water one pint. Infuse twenty minutes.

P. D.—Chamomile half an ounce, water twelve ounces. Infuse fifteen minutes.

Infusum Aurantii.

This is now a simple infusion of orange peel, the lemon peel and clove of former Pharmacopœias being left out; the old infusion differing so much in flavour with the new, must still be used in preparing old prescriptions, or else, as in many other cases, the sick will think there has been some error in the dispensing.

Infusum Bucco.

The same as the Dublin : the difference between it and London and Edinburgh being simply that of troy and avoirdupois weight, and the time of infusing. London had four hours; Edinburgh, two hours; Dublin and British, one hour.

Infusum Calumbæ.

This infusion is now to be made by macerating half an ounce of coarsely powdered calumbo for one hour, with ten fluid ounces of cold water. London had five drachms to a pint of boiling water, and infused for two hours; Edinburgh percolated half an ounce, obtaining sixteen ounces of product; and Dublin macerated three drachms with nine ounces of cold water for two hours.

Infusum Caryophylli.

In this, as in the former infusions, there are differences in the proportions, and the time allowed for infusing. not important in themselves, but still needful for all to notice.

Infusum Cascarillæ.

As the Dublin: one ounce of cascarilla to ten fluid ounces of boiling distilled water. London and Edinburgh had one ounce and a half troy to a pint.

Infusum Catechu.

Would have been the same as London, only there are twenty grains less catechu, and it is to infuse for half an hour instead of an hour. Edinburgh had an addition of syrup, which has been left out; Dublin had one ounce less water, with twenty grains more catechu, the quantity of cinnamon being the same.

Infusum Chiratæ.

Slight variation with Edinburgh and Dublin in point of strength. To be infused with distilled water at 120° for half an hour.

Infusum Cinchonæ Flavæ.

The only bark infusion given now: same proportion as London and Edinburgh, namely, one ounce to a pint, observing only the difference of troy and avoirdupois weight, so often referred to. Dublin used twice that quantity of bark, employing the pale; it is to be filtered through paper, a process hardly necessary, as it will always settle down bright and clear if not required immediately.

Infusum Cuspariæ.

London and Edinburgh employed each five drachms of cusparia to a pint of boiling water; one ounce is now ordered to a pint of water at 120°.

Infusum Cusso.

This is new to the Pharmacopœia: half an ounce of cusso has been commonly given as a dose, infused in half a pint or a pint of boiling water, to expel tape worm.

Infusum Digitalis.

The same strength as London, the spirit of cinnamon being left out; it is only half the strength of Edinburgh and Dublin. This is another case in which the Council have adopted the weaker preparation of a powerful remedy in preference to the stronger.

Infusum Dulcamaræ.

Takes the place of the decoction of the last Pharmacopœias, but differs in strength with all of them. The present has one ounce avoirdupois of dulcamara to ten fluid ounces of water; London had ten drachms troy to a pint of product; Edinburgh and Dublin, one ounce to sixteen of product. The usual dose of the decoction is half an ounce to an ounce, but Dr. Pereira says: " I have often given four ounces for a dose."

Infusum Ergotæ.

The Dublin infusion: using ten ounces of water in place of nine, to a quarter of an ounce of ergot.

Infusum Gentianæ Compositum.

The Edinburgh form, but employing only four hours cold maceration in place of fifteen; it differs essentially with the London, having nearly twice the quantity of gentian, only half the orange peel, and no lemon peel, with an addition of thirty grains of coriander and two ounces of proof spirit in ten ounces. The quantity of gentian is the same as the Dublin, with only one-fourth the quantity of orange peel; there was no lemon peel or coriander in the Dublin. This infusion has one advantage over the former, that it keeps well through the addition of the spirit; and as tinctures are

commonly added to mixtures containing tonic or bitter infusions, prescribers have only to remember, when fixing the
quantity of tincture, that the infusion already contains two
drachms of proof spirit in ten.   The spirit might, I believe,
as I have before stated in the Pharmaceutical Journal, be
added with advantage, and without inconvenience, to many
of the other infusions, viz., orange, calumba, cascarilla, chamomile, and rhubarb.

Infusum Krameriæ.

Similar to London and Dublin, with the exception that
London ordered four hours infusing, and the present one hour.
The proportions are half an ounce of rhatany to ten ounces
of boiling distilled water.

Infusum Lini.

The same as London and Edinburgh, but using twenty
grains less linseed.

Infusum Lupuli.

Approaches closely to the London, but infusing for two
hours only in place of four.

Infusum Maticæ.

Half an ounce of matico to ten fluid ounces of boiling distilled water, as Dublin, but infusing for half-an-hour only in
place of one hour.

Infusum Quassiæ.

This infusion differs with the London and Edinburgh;
same as that of Dublin, excepting the time of infusing, the
relative proportions are as below:—

	Quassia.	Water.	Infuse.
P. B.—	60 grains.	10 oz.	half-an-hour.
P. L.—	20 „	10 oz.	two hours.
P. E.—	30 „	10 oz.	two hours.
P. D.—	54 „	8½ oz.	one hour.

Infusum Rhei.

Rather stronger than the London infusion; only half the
strength of Edinburgh, omitting the spirit of cinnamon; the
same as Dublin, but using ten ounces of water instead of nine.

Infusum Rosæ Acidum.

The Dublin preparation, infusing half-an-hour instead of an hour. The sugar of London and Edinburgh is left out; the proportions of rose petals and acid differing but slightly.

Infusum Senegæ.

Approaches closely to the Dublin, there being but a difference of one ounce of water. The London decoction and the Edinburgh infusion had five drachms of senega in the ten ounces, in place of half an ounce, as now.

Infusum Sennæ.

The alteration in this infusion is very important, in respect to the infusions of London more especially, and Edinburgh: it contains only half the quantity of senna, and ten grains less ginger than London; it has also one-third less senna, and ten grains less ginger than Edinburgh: the proportions are those of Dublin—so that one ounce of this aperient infusion is equal only to half an ounce of London and two-thirds of an ounce of Edinburgh.

Infusum Serpentariæ.

Half an ounce of serpentary, as before, to a pint, and infused for two hours instead of four.

Infusum Uvæ Ursi.

As the London decoction, an ounce to a pint; infuse for two hours. Dublin decoction had one ounce to sixteen ounces of strained product.

Infusum Valerianæ.

One hundred and twenty grains infused with ten ounces of boiling water for an hour. London had the same infused for half-an-hour; Dublin the same, with nine ounces of water, infused for one hour.

Iodum.

Iodine of commerce purified by sublimation, according to Dublin process.

Jalapæ Resina.

A strong tincture of jalap is prepared by exhausting the root with rectified spirit, water is then to be added, and the

D

spirit distilled off, and the residue, while hot, poured into an open dish, and when cold, having poured off the supernatant liquor, the resin is to be washed two or three times with hot water and dried. Parrish recommends the jalap to be digested and boiled with several portions of water, and having thus got rid of the dark-coloured aqueous extract, the pressed root is to be digested with successive portions of alcohol, the tinctures mixed, well shaken with animal charcoal, and filtered ; the greater portion of the spirit to be recovered by distillation, and the remainder evaporated to dryness, the product being nearly colourless.

Linimentum Aconiti.

A strong tincture of the root of aconite prepared by per-colation : one fluid ounce representing one ounce of root, and one pint containing one ounce of camphor in solution ; the loss of spirit is about one-third.

Linimentum Ammoniæ.

Same as the Dublin, having one fluid ounce of liquor ammoniæ to three fluid ounces of olive oil. London and Edinburgh had one to two.

Linimentum Belladonnæ.

Prepared as linimentum aconiti : this preparation contains the value of one ounce of root in each fluid ounce, and where it is desirable to use belladonna in the form of liniment, is much preferable to the extract, as the extract never mixes well with the usual component parts of liniments. This preparation is miscible with spirit, soap liniment, tincture of opium, chloroform, and compound camphor liniment, in any proportion. One part of this liniment may be used with three parts of soap liniment as an external application, to relieve pain—it may also be employed as it is without dilution.

Linimentum Calcis.

Equal parts of oil and solution of lime as before ; all using olive oil with the exception of the Edinburgh, and there linseed oil was ordered.

Linimentum Camphoræ.

One ounce of camphor to four fluid ounces of olive oil ; the same as the last Pharmacopœias of London, Edinburgh, and Dublin.

Linimentum Camphoræ Compositum.

Same proportions as the Dublin, with nearly twice the quantity of ammonia that the London had.

Linimentum Cantharidis.

This is new to the Pharmacopœia : four ounces of powdered cantharides are to be macerated with two fluid ounces of acetic acid for twenty-four hours, then placed in a percolator and æther allowed to pass slowly through, until ten fluid ounces are obtained. The loss of æther in making small quantities is about one-third. This preparation will produce a perfect blister, and therefore must not be used as a liniment, or confused with the Dublin liniment, composed of cantharides and olive oil. Liniment of cantharides does not seem to be the right name.

Linimentum Chloroformi.

This is a new form in the Pharmacopœia, being equal parts, by measure, of chloroform and camphor liniment.

Linimentum Crotonis.

The same proportion as the Dublin, but using olive oil instead of oil of turpentine.

Linimentum Hydrargyri.

The form of the Dublin Pharmacopœia: more readily prepared, and without the loss of so much solution of ammonia as in making the London liniment; the relative strengths of mercurial ointment and solution of ammonia being the same.

Linimentum Iodi.

This is a very strong solution of iodine, with a small quantity of iodide of potassium in rectified spirit—used externally.

Linimentum Opii.

Now contains twice as much tincture of opium as the London did, and the same quantity of opium as Edinburgh and Dublin.

Linimentum Saponis.

This liniment differs with that of each of the last three Pharmacopœias: with London, it differs in the quantity of oil of rosemary, having now three fluid drachms, whereas before it had only fifteen minims in the pint. The Edinburgh had no water in it, and thus far it differed with the present; the Dublin directed proof spirit to be used, and no oil of rosemary; it is to be digested at a temperature not exceeding 70°, with occasional agitation, until all are dissolved. It may not be amiss to mention in this place, that the ordering of English oil of rosemary has caused some surprise amongst pharmaceutical and other chemists; but upon referring to the P. L. " Materia Medica " of 1851, it will be seen that English oil of rosemary is there defined as the kind to be used; but, unfortunately, there is no quantity at all adequate to anything like the possible demand, and I am told, upon reliable authority, that probably there never has been, and never will be; in such a dilemma, it only remains to use the best that can be obtained.

Linimentum Terebinthinæ.

This is very different to the London preparation, having neither soft soap nor camphor; like the Dublin, it has five fluid ounces of oil of turpentine, mixed with eight ounces of resin ointment, remembering that the resin ointment is now differently prepared, which will be noticed in its proper place. The Edinburgh had five fluid ounces of oil of turpentine, four ounces of resin ointment, and one ounce of camphor.

Linimentum Terebinthinæ Aceticum.

Composed of equal portions of oil of turpentine, acetic acid, and camphor liniment.

Liquor Ammoniæ.

One part, by measure, of strong solution of ammonia, and two of distilled water.

P. B.—Specific gravity, 0·959.
P. L.   „   0·960.
P. E.   „   0·960.
P. D.   „   0·950.

Liquor Ammoniæ Acetatis.

This preparation is now very different to any of the former:

it being composed of strong solution of ammonia, saturated with acetic acid, it may be called a concentrated mindererus spirit; and it should be remembered that one ounce is equal to about five ounces of the old preparation: it has this advantage for travellers, that they can carry a good supply in a small compass.

Liquor Ammoniæ Fortior.

Prepared by distillation, hydrochlorate of ammonia being decomposed by slaked lime; for general purposes, this is always made by wholesale manufacturing chemists. The specific gravities, as given below, will show a slight variation :—

P. B.—Specific gravity, 0·891.
P. L.   „   0·882.
P. E.   „   0·880.
P. D.   „   0·900.

Liquor Antimonii Terchloridi.

This is the Dublin preparation, and the principal use is in making the oxide of antimony; it does not represent the butter of antimony of commerce.

Liquor Arsenicalis.

The same as London and Edinburgh, having eighty grains of arsenic in twenty ounces, or four grains to the ounce. The Dublin had two grains more to the pint, with half an ounce of compound tincture of lavender, in place of five drachms.

Liquor Atropiæ.

New to the Pharmacopœia: four grains to the ounce, its chief use being to dilate the pupil of the eye.

Liquor Calcis.

The quantity of lime ordered to be used varies; but as the water dissolves only a limited amount, about eleven grains to the pint, at ordinary temperatures, it is not of importance.

Liquor Calcis Chloratæ.

This is prepared according to the Dublin directions, by well mixing a pound of chlorinated lime with a gallon of distilled water, and after three hours' straining it through calico. This is the disinfecting solution of chloride of lime.

Liquor Calcis Saccharatus.

This is a new Pharmacopœia preparation: the property which sugar possesses of increasing the solubility of lime has been noticed for some time by Mons. Trousseau and others. A fluid drachm should contain about one grain of lime, and the dose of the solution would be from one to two fluid drachms, diluted with two or three ounces of water, or milk and water.

Liquor Chlori.

The Dublin proportions of hydrochloric acid and black oxide of manganese have been adopted, differing but slightly from the London. Edinburgh directed chlorine water to be made with muriate of soda, commercial sulphuric acid, and red oxide of lead; it is quickly spoilt, and should be recently prepared: used chiefly as an antiseptic and disinfectant.

Liquor Ferri Perchloridi.

This solution is half the strength of that formed in the first part of the process for making the tinctura ferri sesquichloridi of Dublin.

Liquor Ferri Pernitratis.

This is the Dublin preparation: used as a styptic, and given internally as an astringent in diarrhœa, hæmorrhages from the bowels, uterus, &c. Dose—from five to fifteen minims, in an ounce or two of water, or spiced water.

Liquor Hydrargyri Nitratis Acidus.

Four ounces of mercury dissolved in three fluid ounces and a quarter of nitric acid, and three fluid ounces of water, according to the Dublin Pharmacopœia. This solution must not be used in making the ointment of nitrate of mercury, as upon referring to the form for making the ointment it will be seen that it contains rather less than half the quantity of acid it should do for that purpose.

Liquor Morphiæ Hydrochloratis.

This solution, it is necessary to observe, only contains four grains of the hydrochlorate of morphia in the ounce, or half a grain in the drachm, just half the strength of the London Pharmacopœia, but nearly the same as the solutions of the

Edinburgh and Dublin, which had four grains and a half in the ounce, being a shade more than half a grain to the drachm. This is another case where the Council have chosen the weaker preparation of a powerful medicine.

Liquor Plumbi Subacetatis.

This solution resembles the London and Edinburgh so closely as to be almost the same thing, and is nearly twice as strong as the Dublin solution.

Liquor Plumbi Subacetatis Dilutus.

This dilute solution contains half a drachm more of the liquor plumbi subacetatis than the London, and about the same quantity relatively to strength as the Dublin.

Liquor Potassæ.

This liquor is prepared as nearly as possible according to the Dublin process.

Liquor Potassæ Permanganatis.

A solution of four grains of permanganate of potash in one fluid ounce of distilled water, used externally to foul ulcers as a caustic and deodorizer.

Liquor Sodæ.

Using twenty-eight ounces of carbonate of soda with twelve ounces of slaked lime, and one gallon of distilled water, following the directions given for liquor potassæ.

Liquor Sodæ Arseniatis.

A solution of arseniate of soda in the proportion of four grains to the ounce. Dose—same as liquor arsenicalis.

Liquor Sodæ Chloratæ.

This is the preparation of the London Pharmacopœia, used as a disinfectant and antiseptic in the same way as the solution of chlorinated lime. When used as a gargle, it should be diluted with eight or ten parts of water; as an injection, fifteen to thirty; as a lotion, the proportions vary according to circumstances.

Liquor Strychniæ.

Four grains of strychnia in one fluid ounce of the solution. Dose—five minims, equal to $\frac{1}{12}$ of a grain, cautiously increased.

Lithiæ Citras.

A new preparation, given in gout, in five to ten grain doses.

Magnesia.

This is the present carbonate of magnesia calcined, and formerly known as heavy calcined magnesia.

Magnesia Levis.

This is prepared by calcining the light carbonate, and has hitherto been known as magnesia, or calcined magnesia.

Magnesiæ Carbonas.

The Dublin process for preparing what has been known as heavy carbonate of magnesia. The rationale of the process is to have the solutions of carbonate of soda and sulphate of magnesia as near saturation as possible before mixing.

Magnesiæ Carbonas Levis.

This is the Dublin process for making what has hitherto been known as carbonate of magnesia; a larger quantity of water is used in dissolving the sulphate of magnesia and carbonate of soda, and the solutions are to be mixed cold.

Mel Boracis.

Sixty-four grains of borax are ordered with one ounce of clarified honey, making a proportion of eight grains to the eighth part of an ounce; formerly, it was one drachm to one ounce.

Mel Depuratum.

Honey melted in a water-bath, and strained while hot through flannel previously moistened with warm water; some scum always rises, which is usually removed with a spoon.

Mistura Ammoniaci.

The same proportions as before.

Mistura Amygdalæ.

This represents the mistura amygdalæ of London; contains nearly twice the quantity of almonds, gum, and sugar that the Edinburgh did, with a small difference in the quantity of almonds when compared with the Dublin.

Mistura Creasoti.

This is the Edinburgh mixture, but substituting half a fluid drachm of spirit of juniper P.B. instead of one ounce of the compound spirit of juniper P.E.

Mistura Cretæ.

This is prepared as nearly like the mistura cretæ of former Pharmacopœias as possible.

Mistura Ferri Composita.

This preparation is substantially the same as before, remembering that the spirit of nutmeg is the strong spirit of the present P.B., answering to the essence of nutmeg of Dublin, and not the weaker preparation of London or Edinburgh. It may be a matter of surprise to those who know the difference between an emulsion made with powdered myrrh and that made with a carefully-selected piece of gum, that the myrrh in lump was not ordered to be used.

Mistura Guaiaci.

This mixture, with the exception of a very slight variation caused by the change in the weights, is the same as before.

Mistura Scammonii.

The Edinburgh mixture, having two grains of resin of scammony in a fluid ounce of milk, instead of seven grains in three fluid ounces of milk.

Morphiæ Hydrochloras.

The process is similar to that of the Dublin Pharmacopœia; but such preparations are best left in the hands of those who make them their special care.

Mucilago Acaciæ.

The Dublin form has been adopted, being as two to three instead of one to two, as London mistura.

Mucilago Amyli.

The same as the London decoction and Edinburgh mucilage: it has only half the quantity of starch ordered in the Dublin mucilage.

Mucilago Tragacanthæ.

Ten grains of tragacanth to the ounce, rather less than the Edinburgh form, which contained one hundred and twenty grains in nine ounces.

Oxymel.

One part of acetic acid in ten, as nearly as possible the same as London. The Dublin contained more acid, viz., three fluid ounces to sixteen by weight, of honey.

Pilula Aloes Barbadensis.

This is new to the Pharmacopœia, but appears to be a substitute for the pilula aloes cum sapone (commonly known as Marshall Hall's pill); it has one grain of aloes in two grains of the mass.

Pilula Aloes et Assafœtidæ.

The Edinburgh pill, containing one grain of aloes and one of assafœtida in four grains of the mass.

Pilula Aloes et Myrrhæ.

The Edinburgh form, with the quantity of conserve to be used, distinctly stated, containing two grains of aloes in six of the mass; it has half the quantity of saffron contained in the corresponding pill of the London Pharmacopœia.

Pilula Aloes Socotrinæ.

Resembling the Edinburgh pilula aloes, with the addition of volatile oil of nutmeg, and rather more aloes; it contains two grains of socotrine aloes in four of the mass.

Pilula Assafœtidæ Composita.

This pill takes the place of the pilula galbani composita of London, the sagapenum and soap being left out. It resembles the Edinburgh in the use of equal parts of assafœtida, galbanum, and myrrh; but treacle is used instead of conserve of roses in making up the mass. The Dublin form had two parts of assafœtida to one each of galbanum, myrrh, and treacle. The present pill contains two grains of assafœtida in seven.

Pilula Calomelanos Composita.

This is the Dublin pill: it is to be made into a mass with castor oil instead of treacle. It contains one grain of calomel in five; the London and Edinburgh had one in six.

Pilula Cambogiæ Composita.

The Edinburgh form for this pill has been adopted: it contains about one-half the quantity of gamboge, and one-third the quantity of aloes that the London form did; Barbadoes aloes are used in place of socotrine, and aromatic powder instead of ginger. It contains one grain of aloes and one grain of gamboge in six grains of the mass.

Pilula Colocynthidis Composita.

This is the Edinburgh pill, and must not be taken for pilula colocynthidis composita P.L., now represented by the extractum colocynthidis compositum, nor for pilula colcynthidis composita of Dublin; Barbadoes aloes are substituted for socotrine.

Pilula Colocynthidis et Hyoscyami.

The former pill mass with the addition of extract of henbane, in the proportion of one part of extract to two of pill mass.

Pilula Ferri Carbonatis.

The Edinburgh pill, containing four parts of saccharated carbonate of iron to one part of confection of roses.

Pilula Ferri Iodidi.

This is a good form for preparing pills of iodide of iron; in practice, the quantity of water ordered is scarcely sufficient, a five-grain pill will contain about one grain and a third of iodide of iron.

Pilula Hydrargyri.
There is no alteration in this pill.

Pilula Opii.
This is prepared according to the Dublin form, being one part of powdered opium and four parts of hard soap beat into a mass with water. The corresponding pill of London was composed of opium, powdered liquorice root and soft soap; the Edinburgh of opium, sulphate of potash, and conserve of roses. The present pill contains one grain of opium in five, allowing nothing for the water.

Pilula Plumbi cum Opio.
This is the Edinburgh form, and contains one grain of opium combined with six of acetate of lead and one of confection of roses.

Pilula Rhei Composita.
The most important change in this pill, as regards London, is the substitution of oil of peppermint for oil of caraway, and hard soap is now ordered in the place of soft soap. As regards Edinburgh, treacle takes the place of conserve of roses, and there is less oil of peppermint; the aperient quality remains about the same.

Pilula Scillæ Composita.
This pill contains about one-fifth more squill, and only half the quantity of ginger and ammoniac that the London did, with hard soap and treacle in place of soft soap and treacle. It agrees with the Edinburgh and Dublin forms, with but two minor exceptions: the Edinburgh ordered conserve of roses in place of treacle, and Dublin ordered only half the quantity of the latter ingredient.

Plumbi Acetas.
Litharge dissolved in acetic acid and water by the aid of heat, filtered, evaporated, and crystallized, similar to the Edinburgh process.

Podophylli Resina.

The process given for preparing this resin is similar to that found in Parrish's "Practical Pharmacy." Podophyllin was introduced into this country rather more than ten years ago, but has been but little employed till within the last four or five years. It is an active aperient, but is seldom given alone, but combined with other aperients, such as rhubarb, jalap, or colocynth. The dose is from a quarter of a grain to two grains; in the larger dose it is apt to produce nausea and griping, more especially if given uncombined.

Potassa Caustica.

Solution of potash evaporated rapidly in a silver, or clean iron vessel, and poured into pencil-shaped moulds.

Potassa Sulphurata.

Carbonate of potash and sublimed sulphur mixed together in a warm mortar, and heated in a crucible until perfect fusion has taken place, then to be poured upon a stone and quickly covered, and when cold to be broken into pieces and kept in air-tight stoppered bottles. Used as a lotion or ointment in some diseases of the skin, in the proportion of half an ounce to a quart of water, or half a drachm to an ounce of cerate.

Potassæ Acetas.

Carbonate of potash dissolved in acetic acid and filtered, slightly acidulated, if necessary, with a few additional drops of acid, and having evaporated to dryness in a thin porcelain basin, and cautiously raised the heat so as to liquefy the product, allow the basin to cool, and when the salt has solidified, while still warm, break it into fragments, and put it into stoppered bottles. Used as a diuretic in dropsy, in doses of twenty to sixty grains in solution.

Potassæ Bicarbonas.

A process is given for preparing this salt. For all ordinary purposes for which it is required, it is prepared by manufacturers upon a large scale.

Potassæ Chloras.

The process is similar to one given in Muspratt's "Chemistry" as an economical mode of preparing this salt. Chlorine is to be passed into a mixture of carbonate of potash and slaked lime, which is afterwards to be boiled for twenty minutes with water, then filtered and crystallized, and the crystals purified by solution in three times their weight of boiling distilled water, and the solution then allowed to crystallize. It has been much prescribed of late years as a saline alterative, and is supposed to impart oxygen to the system; but medical writers are much divided in their opinion respecting its action: it is frequently ordered in gargles instead of nitrate of potash, in the proportion of sixty grains to half a pint. Dose—internally, five grains to thirty in solution.

Potassæ Citras.

This is now placed among the Pharmacopœia preparations for the first time: it is prepared by mixing filtered solutions of citric acid and carbonate of potash, and evaporating to dryness, stirring constantly after a pellicle has formed: a cooling saline. Dose—thirty grains to a quarter of an ounce, in solution.

Potassæ Nitras.

Commercial nitrate of potash dissolved in boiling distilled water, granulated by stirring until cold, and washed with cold distilled water in a percolator, until the liquid which passes through ceases to give a precipitate, with a solution of nitrate of silver. In the first part of the directions, straining the hot solution, which would generally be contaminated with dirt, appears to have been overlooked.

Potassæ Permanganas.

This salt is obtained in purple crystals, soluble in sixteen parts of distilled water: used in making the liquor potassæ permanganatis; employed externally, by dusting in powder, upon foul ulcers, as a caustic and deodorizer.

Potassæ Sulphas.

This salt (commonly known as sal polychrest) is ordered to be prepared according to the process given in the Dublin Pharmacopœia.

Potassæ Tartras.

This salt is to be prepared by adding acid tartrate of potash (bitartrate of potash) to a solution of carbonate of potash boiling, neutralizing perfectly, filtering, evaporating, and crystallizing.

Potassii Bromidum.

The salt is now prepared by adding bromine to a solution of potash, evaporating the solution to dryness, powdering the residue, and mixing intimately with charcoal, and then submitting it to a red heat, throwing small quantities at a time into the crucible, and when brought into a state of fusion the contents of the crucible are to be poured out. The fused mass having become cold, it is to be dissolved in water, and the solution filtered and crystallized. Use: the same as iodide of potassium. Dose—five grains to fifteen.

Potassii Iodidum.

This salt is to be prepared in a manner similar to that of the bromide of potassium; but these salts are made profitably only upon a large scale.

Pulvis Amygdalæ Compositus.

This is the confectio amygdalæ of London, and the conserva amygdalæ of Edinburgh in a dry state. Proportion for mistura amygdalæ—fifty-four grains to an ounce, or one ounce to eight.

Pulvis Antimonialis.

One ounce of oxide of antimony, and two ounces of precipitated phosphate of lime, thoroughly mixed: this is an improvement upon the burning of horn shavings and tersulphuret of antimony, of London and Edinburgh. Dose—five to ten grains.

Pulvis Aromaticus.

This powder is intended, when mixed with prepared chalk, to represent the confectio aromatica of London, and must not therefore be mistaken for the former pulvis aromaticus of Edinburgh and Dublin, or pulvis cinnamomi compositus of London, now no longer recognized.

Pulvis Catechu Compositus.

This powder is taken from the Dublin Pharmacopœia, omitting half the quantity of kino there ordered, and putting in the place thereof an equal quantity of rhatany powder. This is a good astringent powder. Dose—five to thirty grains.

Pulvis Cretæ Aromaticus.

This is the representative of the confectio aromatica of London, and, though very similar in taste, contains a much larger quantity of the aromatics, and that inert expensive article, saffron. The two forms are compared as follows :—

P. B.			P. L.	
Cinnamon	4 oz.	Cinnamon	2 oz.
Nutmeg	3 oz.	Nutmeg	2 oz.
Saffron	3 oz.	Saffron	2 oz.
Cloves	1½ oz.	Cloves	1 oz.
Cardamoms	1 oz.	Cardamoms	¼ oz.
Sugar	25 oz.	Sugar	24 oz.
Chalk	12½ oz.	Chalk	16 oz.
3 lbs. 2 oz.		**2 lbs. 15¼ oz.**	

It will thus be seen that the new preparation contains nearly twice the quantity of cinnamon, and half as much more of the other aromatics and saffron as the old one.

Pulvis Cretæ Aromaticus cum Opio.

This powder is different to the pulvis cretæ compositus cum opio of London, as it contains no tormentil, pepper, or gum arabic, but is a compound of pulvis cretæ aromaticus and powdered opium : it contains one grain of opium in forty grains.

Pulvis Ipecacuanhæ cum Opio.

There is no alteration in the proportions of this powder : it contains one grain of opium in ten.

Pulvis Jalapæ Compositus.

This powder has rather more ginger than the London had, and rather less than the Dublin ; Edinburgh had no ginger ; the proportion of jalap remains the same, namely, one part in three.

Pulvis Kino cum Opio.

There is no alteration in this preparation, it being that of the London Pharmacopœia : it contains one grain of opium in twenty.

Pulvis Rhei Compositus.

The rhubarb, magnesia, and ginger powder of Edinburgh and Dublin. Dose—as a stomachic antacid aperient, thirty to sixty grains.

Pulvis Scammonii Compositus.

This is after the London form, substituting powdered jalap for extract : it contains one grain of scammony in two of the powder.

Pulvis Tragacanthæ Compositus.

This powder now contains one-third more sugar than the former of London and Edinburgh.

Quiniæ Sulphas.

The manufacture of this substance is confined entirely to those who make it their especial business.

Resina Scammonii.

The resin extracted from the root by maceration and percolation with spirit, and precipitated therefrom by the addition of water. Dose—five grains ; generally given in combination with other aperients ; seldom given alone.

Santoninum.

This substance is new to the Pharmacopœia. A detailed process is given for preparing it. It is much employed in America and upon the Continent as a vermifuge for children. The dose of santonine varies from one to tei grains at bed-time, or in the form of lozenges, containing two grains each, three times a day, followed by an aperient in the morning.

Soda Caustica.

New to the Pharmacopœia. Prepared as potassa caustica, but not ordered to be moulded.

Sodæ Arsenias.

This preparation is also new to the Pharmacopœia, although it has long been in use in those forms of disease where the employment of arsenic is desirable. Dose—$\frac{1}{16}$ of a grain in solution with water, or spiced water, and some aromatic tincture.

E

Sodæ Bicarbonas.

This is a very extensive article of commerce, and like some others, is made upon a very large scale; its daily uses are so well understood that it is not necessary to enter into particulars concerning them.

Sodæ Carbonas Exsiccata.

Carbonate of soda dried by exposure to a strong heat and afterwards powdered: it is very little used.

Sodæ et Potassæ Tartras.

This salt is to be prepared by adding the acid tartrate of potash to the carbonate of soda dissolved in water, and proceeding as in making tartrate of potash. The process given is similar to that of Edinburgh.

Sodæ Phosphas.

The process for making this salt (known as tasteless salts) is similar to that described in the Dublin Pharmacopœia. In doses of half an ounce to an ounce; it acts as an aperient taken in plenty of water.

Spiritus Ætheris.

This is the Edinburgh preparation, being a mixture of æther and rectified spirit, omitting the oleum æthereum of London.

Spiritus Ætheris Nitrosi.

A new process is now given for preparing this old-established medicine, under the impression, it would seem, that a more definite and reliable product would result than from the old plan. This preparation, in respect to the process, has already raised some discussion, and probably will cause much more. The dose remains the same as the spiritus ætheris nitrici of old.

Spiritus Ammoniæ Aromaticus.

This preparation has undergone some considerable change with respect to the aromatics, on account of the dark colour which the old kind always assumed after it had been made some little time. As now prepared, it is a solution of carbonate of ammonia in spirit and water combined with volatile oil of nutmeg and oil of lemon. It now contains six pints of rectified spirit in seven of the preparation, whereas, in the London, it only had four pints of spirit in six; the cinnamon and cloves are now left out. The preparations of Edinburgh and Dublin were solutions of caustic ammonia, the volatile oil of rosemary of Edinburgh and oil of cinnamon of Dublin are omitted. The dose is thirty to sixty minims in a wine-glassful of water.

Spiritus Armoraciæ Compositus.

The London preparation as before, with sixty grains less nutmeg, and remembering avoirdupois, loco troy weight.

Spiritus Cajuputi.

In this and most of the following spirits it is necessary to observe that they are totally different to the spirits of the London and Edinburgh Pharmacopœias; they are, in fact, in most instances, the essences of the Dublin Pharmacopœia. This spirit of cajeput is a fresh introduction to the Pharmacopœia; it contains one part, by measure, of oil of cajeput with nine of rectified spirit; it is used externally as an adjunct to liniments in rheumatism; and internally to allay spasms and sickness, in doses of ten to thirty minims, diluted.

Spiritus Camphoræ.

This spirit contains rather less camphor than the spirit of the last Pharmacopœias. It has one ounce avoirdupois of camphor to nine fluid ounces of spirit, the others had one ounce to eight.

Spiritus Chloroformi.

This is new to the Pharmacopœia, and probably intended to take the place of the so-called chloric æther; but this spirit is not half the strength of that which has hitherto been used under the name of chloric æther, or spirit of chloric æther. The dose of spirit of chloroform is from ten to thirty minims, diluted.

Spiritus Juniperi.

This spirit contains about ninety times the quantity of oil of juniper that the three last preparations of juniper did. It is made with rectified spirit instead of proof, and the fennel and caraway are left out.

Spiritus Lavandulæ.

Simple spirit of lavender, containing one fluid ounce of oil of lavender in ten.

Spiritus Menthæ Piperitæ.

This spirit has about forty-five times as much oil as the London had, and is made with rectified spirit in place of proof. The Edinburgh was made with the fresh herb.

Spiritus Myristicæ.

One part of oil to nine of rectified spirit. The London and Edinburgh ordered two ounces and a half of nutmegs, and a gallon of proof spirit to be distilled off.

Spiritus Rosmarini.

This spirit contains about sixty-four times as much oil as the London spirit. The Edinburgh was distilled from fresh rosemary.

Spiritus Tenuior.

The same as London: five of rectified spirit to three of water—S.G. 0·920. Edinburgh had two of spirit to one of water—S.G. 0·912. Dublin, seven to four—S.G. 0·920.

Strychnia.

This powerfully-poisonous alkaloid will necessarily be prepared only by those manufacturers who make it one of their special articles.

Succus Conii.

The juice of the fresh leaves with rectified spirit in the proportion of three fluid parts of juice to one of spirit. Dose —fifteen to sixty minims.

Succus Scoparii.

Prepared as succus conii. Dose — one to four fluid drachms.

Succus Taraxaci.

One measure of rectified spirit to three measures of juice expressed from the fresh root. Dose — one to six fluid drachms.

Sulphur Præcipitatum.

The process for making precipitated sulphur, or milk of sulphur, as commonly designated, is now for the first time given in the Pharmacopœia. Sublimed sulphur and slaked lime are to be boiled together with distilled water; to the filtered solution sufficient hydrochloric acid is to be added to precipitate the whole of the sulphur, which is to be collected, washed, and dried. Its uses are the same as those of sublimed sulphur.

Suppositoria Acidi Tannici.

This is a new feature in the Pharmacopœia; each suppository contains two grains of tannin, or tannic acid.

Suppositoria Morphiæ.

Each suppository should contain a quarter of a grain of hydrochlorate of morphia.

Syrupus.

Proportions same as before; adding water, if necessary, to bring the syrup to the proper weight.

Syrupus Aurantii.

To be made with the tincture of orange-peel in the proportion of one ounce of tincture to seven of syrup. This is a ready way of making the syrup. It is not quite so dark, nor so strongly flavoured.

Syrupus Aurantii Floris.

A new syrup in Pharmacopœia. Much in use on the Continent. Hitherto a little orange-flower water, added to a mixture or draught, has answered.

Syrupus Ferri Iodidi.

This syrup is to be prepared in a way similar to that ordered in the London Pharmacopœia, only that the syrup is now to be brought to a given weight, and not measure, as last ordered. One fluid drachm should contain about five grains of iodide of iron.

Syrupus Ferri Phosphatis.

This syrup is new to the Pharmacopœia, though a syrup of the superphosphate has been long in use. Possibly this preparation may prove a more stable compound; if it should, it will be an acquisition. Dose—one to four drachms.

Syrupus Hemidesmi.

Syrup of Indian sarsaparilla. This is the Dublin form. It is much too weak to be of any use beyond flavour or colour.

Syrupus Limonis.

The syrup of London, with the addition of lemon peel, to increase the flavour, but omitting the spirit.

Syrupus Mori.

The London syrup, principally used for sweetening.

Syrupus Papaveris.

This syrup is the same strength as that prepared according to the London process; but there is a difference in the *modus operandi.* After macerating the poppies in a water-bath for twelve hours, all the water is to be evaporated except that absorbed by the broken capsules, which is to be strongly pressed out and strained, and being reduced to the prescribed quantity, when cold, the spirit is to be added, and being well mixed, to be filtered; the spirit is then to be distilled off, the liquor reduced to two pints, and the sugar added. This process is more troublesome than the old one, necessitating the possession of a still for every one attempting to make his own syrup of poppies.

Syrupus Rhœados.

This is prepared as the London, bringing the syrup, when finished, to a given weight and specific gravity—1·330.

Syrupus Rosæ Gallicæ.

This syrup takes the place of the syrupus rosæ, made with the centifolia rose. It is prepared according to the Edinburgh form, with half as much more sugar. It may be used *ad libitum.*

Syrupus Scillæ.

Similar to the syrupus scillæ of Edinburgh. Dose—a fluid drachm.

Syrupus Sennæ.

This syrup is unlike either the London or Edinburgh preparation; sugar is now used instead of treacle, the manna of London is omitted, and oil of coriander substituted for fennel. One fluid ounce of this syrup has the value of about half an ounce of senna-leaves.

Syrupus Tolutanus.

Prepared with the balsam of tolu, as the London, and not with tincture, as the Edinburgh.

Syrupus Zingiberis.

Prepared by adding one ounce of tincture of ginger to seven ounces of simple syrup, according to the Dublin form.

N.B.—In making the following tinctures, all those which are to be prepared by percolation, after as much of the tincture as will, has percolated through, the contents of the percolator are to be pressed, the tincture added to that already obtained, and the original measure is to be made up either by proof or rectified spirit, as the case may be:—

Tinctura Aconiti.

Prepared from the root by maceration and percolation, with rectified spirit. This tincture has only one-third the strength of that of London, and one-fourth of that of Dublin. Used externally, to allay neuralgic pains. Dose—internally, ten minims, administered with caution.

Tinctura Aloes.

This tincture has the same proportion of aloes and liquorice as the London and Edinburgh, but proof spirit is now directed to be used, instead of a pint and a half of water with half a pint of spirit. One fluid ounce should contain about ten grains of aloes.

Tinctura Arnicæ.

This tincture is new to the Pharmacopœia, although it has been for many years in use, and arnica had a place in the Materia Medica of London, 1787, although subsequently abandoned; it is now again brought forward. Various opinions are entertained as to its efficacy; it is said to accelerate the pulse when taken internally, and act as a tonic and diuretic. The dose of the tincture will be one or two fluid drachms; externally, as a lotion to bruises, it is used in various proportions, from one part of the tincture to fifteen of water, to equal parts: it is prepared by maceration and percolation.

Tinctura Assafœtidæ.

This tincture remains the same, excepting always the difference between troy and avoirdupois weight.

Tinctura Aurantii.

The same strength as Dublin, contains a little more orange-peel than the London and Edinburgh, prepared by maceration and percolation.

Tinctura Belladonnæ.

By macerating the dried leaves, coarsely powdered, in proof spirit, and percolating. It has rather less than half the strength of the London and Dublin tincture. Dose—ten to twenty minims.

Tinctura Benzoini Composita.

Similar to that of London, storax and tolu taking the place of peru balsam of the Edinburgh.

Tinctura Bucco.

The same as Edinburgh and Dublin: two ounces and a half to a pint of proof spirit, prepared by maceration and percolation.

Tinctura Calumbæ.

Prepared by maceration and percolation: this tincture contains rather over a third more of calumbo than London and Edinburgh, and is the same strength as the Dublin.

Tinctura Camphoræ cum Opio.

This tincture contains two grains of opium in the fluid ounce, and resembles the tinctura camphoræ composita of London so closely as to be almost identical.

Tinctura Cannabis Indicæ.

The same as the Dublin: it contains nearly three grains of the extract in a fluid drachm. Dose—ten to thirty minims.

Tinctura Cantharidis.

No change in this tincture: prepared by maceration and percolation.

Tinctura Capsici.

This tincture is about the same strength as the London and Edinburgh, but only half the strength of Dublin: prepared by maceration and percolation. One cannot help remarking, that in this and the previous tincture, a quarter of an ounce of material in one case, and three quarters of an ounce in the other, are to be macerated with fifteen ounces of spirit before percolating, the same quantity as directed for four ounces of powdered bark, in preparing the tincture of that substance.

Tinctura Cardamomi Composita.

The quantities of the aromatics are somewhat increased, and the colouring matter decreased, when compared with the London. To be macerated and percolated.

Tinctura Cascarillæ.

The same proportions as before: prepared by maceration and percolation.

Tinctura Castorei.

This tincture has a quarter of an ounce less castor to the pint than that of London or Edinburgh.

Tinctura Catechu.

To be prepared by maceration and percolation: it has about one-fourth more catechu and one-fourth less cinnamon than the corresponding tincture of London and Edinburgh.

Tinctura Chiratæ.

The Dublin tincture, prepared by maceration and percolation. Dose—ten to sixty minims.

Tinctura Cinchonæ Composita.

The proportions for this tincture are, with a slight difference in the quantity of orange-peel, the same as before.   The Edinburgh ordered yellow bark and not pale : prepared by maceration and percolation.

Tinctura Cinchonæ.

Proportions as before.   Process—maceration and percolation.

Tinctura Cinnamomi.

Contains about a fourth more cinnamon than the tincture of London and Edinburgh.   Process—maceration and percolation.

Tinctura Cocci.

Same as the Dublin ; allowing half an ounce of cochineal for the spirit added, to make a full pint when finished.

Tinctura Colchici Seminis.

Prepared by maceration and percolation.   Dose—from twenty to thirty minims.

Tinctura Conii Fructus.

Tincture of the hemlock fruit is now ordered to be prepared instead of tincture of the leaves.   It is made by maceration and percolation.   The dose is from thirty minims upwards.

Tinctura Croci.

This tincture is introduced into the P.B., while the syrup is omitted.   It is prepared by maceration and percolation. It is the strength of the Edinburgh, and half the strength of the Dublin ; principally used for colouring.

Tinctura Digitalis.

Prepared by maceration and percolation.   This closely resembles the tinctures of London, Edinburgh, and Dublin in strength ; for, though the quantity of leaves employed is five ounces to two pints against four ounces of London and Edinburgh, yet the difference between troy and avoirdupois weight, and the making up the product by the addition of proof spirit to the full measure ordered, make the result so similar that the dose does not require altering.

Tinctura Ergotæ.

Prepared by maceration and percolation with proof spirit. It contains a third less ergot than the London æthereal tincture, and the same quantity as the Dublin spirituous tincture. One fluid ounce represents a quarter of an ounce of ergot. The dose will therefore be one fluid drachm and upwards.

Tinctura Ferri Perchloridi.

This represents as closely as possible the tinctura ferri sesquichloridi of London, and is only about one-fourth the strength of the Dublin tincture. Dose—ten to thirty minims, diluted.

Tinctura Gallæ.

Prepared by maceration and percolation. Principally used as a test.

Tinctura Gentianæ Composita.

Prepared by maceration and percolation. The quantity of cardamom is rather less as regards London; the canella and cochineal of Edinburgh are omitted.

Tinctura Guaiaci Ammoniata.

As regards London, there is no change in this tincture; but Edinburgh employed simple spirit of ammonia.

Tinctura Hyoscyami.

This tincture is rather weaker than that of London and Edinburgh, about one-tenth, not sufficient to affect the dose. It is prepared by maceration and percolation.

Tinctura Iodi.

This tincture differs with the tinctures of iodine which have preceded it. It has the same quantity of iodine as the London, with only one-fourth of the iodide of potassium; it has three-fifths less iodine than the Edinburgh, which contained no iodide of potassium; it contains the same amount of iodine as the Dublin, with one-fourth the iodide of potassium. Dose—ten minims, gradually increased, if necessary; may be given in sherry, if wine be admissible.

Tinctura Jalapæ.

This tincture is not quite so strong of jalap as the London, and is about one-third weaker than that of Edinburgh and Dublin. It is prepared by maceration and percolation.

Tinctura Kino.

The same proportions as nearly as possible as the London and Edinburgh. If this tincture, when filtered, is put into two-ounce bottles, it will keep without gelatinizing.

Tinctura Krameriæ.

This tincture is little more than half the strength of the Dublin. It is prepared by maceration and percolation. Used as an astringent for the gums. Dose internally—one to two fluid drachms.

Tinctura Lavandulæ Composita.

This is the tincture of the London Pharmacopœia. The cloves of the Edinburgh are left out; and it has only half the lavender and one-tenth of the rosemary, and none of the cloves or cochineal of Dublin.

Tinctura Limonis.

It has rather more lemon than the London had. It is the same strength as the Dublin. Prepared by maceration and percolation. Used for flavouring.

Tinctura Lobeliæ.

Prepared by maceration and percolation. The same strength as the tinctures of the three previous Pharmacopœias. Dose—ten to sixty minims.

Tinctura Lobeliæ Ætherea.

Prepared by maceration : proportions the same as before. Dose—ten to sixty minims.

Tinctura Lupuli.

This tincture has about a fourth less hop than the London, and is about one-fifth of the strength of the tinctures of Edinburgh and Dublin, which were prepared with lupulin.

Tinctura Myrrhæ.

This tincture has more myrrh than either of the three previous tinctures of myrrh. It has five ounces avoirdupois to two pints. London had three ounces troy, Edinburgh three ounces and a half troy, and Dublin four ounces avoirdupois, to two pints. Prepared by maceration and percolation.

Tinctura Nucis Vomicæ.

No form for this tincture has been given since the Dublin of 1826, which had two ounces of nux vomica to eight ounces of rectified spirit, the present having two ounces only to twenty of spirit; it is therefore rather less than half the strength. It is prepared by maceration and percolation. The dose is from ten to twenty minims.

Tinctura Opii.

The proportions for this tincture bear very closely upon those of London, Edinburgh, and Dublin; but in consequence of the change of weight, and the additional quantity of proof spirit to make up the full measure as directed, the present tincture is rather weaker than the previous ones, as thus—the value of one grain of powdered opium is contained in fifteen minims of the P.B. tincture, the same value was contained in thirteen minims of the L. or E.P. or D.P. The E.P. used sliced, not powdered opium.

Tinctura Quiniæ Composita.

The same as the L.P.

Tinctura Rhei.

The present tincture is different to any of its predecessors. It has about one-fourth more rhubarb than the London, cardamoms and coriander in the place of liquorice and ginger; it has the same quantity of rhubarb as the Edinburgh, with the addition of coriander and saffron; it has about one-fourth more rhubarb than the Dublin, half the quantity of cardamoms, and no liquorice. It is prepared by maceration and percolation. Dose—as a stomachic, one fluid drachm: purgative, an ounce to an ounce and a half.

Tinctura Sabinæ.

This tincture is new to the Pharmacopœia. Prepared by maceration and percolation. One fluid ounce represents one-eighth of an ounce of savine. The dose for internal use would be from twenty to sixty minims.

Tinctura Scillæ.

It is about one-tenth weaker than the former tinctures of squill, in consequence of the loss in the product being made up by proof spirit.

Tinctura Senegæ.

This tincture is new to the Pharmacopœia. Dose—as a stimulant and expectorant, from thirty minims to two fluid drachms. Prepared by maceration and percolation.

Tinctura Sennæ.

This tincture resembles that of London and Dublin in its aperient quality; but it contains half the caraway, and coriander is substituted for cardamoms. It has neither the sugar nor jalap of Edinburgh, and about half the quantity of senna. It is prepared by maceration and percolation.

Tinctura Serpentariæ.

This tincture resembles that of London, the cochineal of Edinburgh being left out. It is prepared by maceration and percolation.

Tinctura Stramonii.

This is the Dublin preparation, employing maceration and percolation in making it. Dose—ten to twenty minims.

Tinctura Tolutana.

This tincture contains nearly twice and a half the quantity of tolu that the London did, and about a fifth more than Edinburgh and Dublin.

Tinctura Valerianæ.

There is no material difference in the strength of this and former tinctures of valerian. Prepared by maceration and percolation.

Tinctura Valerianæ Ammoniata.

Same as the preceding, employing aromatic spirit of ammonia in place of proof spirit. Edinburgh used spiritus ammoniæ.

Tinctura Zingiberis.

This tincture has nearly twice the strength of the London and Edinburgh, and rather more than half the strength of the Dublin. Prepared by maceration and percolation.

Trochisci Acidi Tannici.

These as well as all the following lozenges are new to the London and Dublin Pharmacopœias; the tannin, bismuth, and catechu are also new to Edinburgh, but not the morphia, morphia and ipecacuanha, and opium, which are taken from the Edinburgh. Each lozenge contains half a grain of tannin, and should weigh about fifteen grains.

Trochisci Bismuthi.

Each lozenge contains two grains of bismuth, combined with carbonate of magnesia and carbonate of lime.

Trochisci Catechu.

Each lozenge contains about a grain and a quarter of catechu.

Trochisci Morphiæ.

Each lozenge should contain one-thirty-sixth of a grain of hydrochlorate of morphia, and weigh fifteen and a half grains.

Trochisci Morphiæ et Ipecacuanhæ.

Each lozenge should contain one-thirty-sixth of a grain of hydrochlorate of morphia and one-twelfth of a grain of ipecacuanha, and weigh about fifteen grains.

Trochisci Opii.

Each lozenge should contain one-tenth of a grain of extract of opium, and should weigh about twelve grains. These lozenges, as well as the morphia, require much care in their employment, and should be kept out of the reach of children.

Unguentum Aconitiæ.

This ointment is used chiefly in neuralgic affections. It contains one grain of aconitia in the eighth part of an ounce.

Unguentum Antimonii Tartarati.

This ointment contains the same relative proportions as London and Edinburgh—namely, one part to four: it has nearly twice the quantity of tartarated antimony as the Dublin. Simple ointment is introduced as a substitute for lard.

Unguentum Atropiæ.

This ointment is new to the Pharmacopœia. Use—to smear over the upper eyelid, to dilate the pupil.

Unguentum Belladonnæ.

This ointment, as compared with that of London, has eighty grains to the ounce instead of sixty.

Unguentum Calomelanos.

This ointment is new to the Pharmacopœia, and has ten grains of calomel in the eighth part of an ounce.

Unguentum Cantharidis.

The cantharides are to be digested in the oil in a covered vessel for twelve hours, and then at 212° temperature for fifteen minutes, then strained, pressed, and added to the wax previously melted. One ounce contains the value of one-eighth of an ounce of cantharides.

Unguentum Cetacei.

The same proportions as London, using almond oil in place of olive, to keep it white.

Unguentum Cocculi.

This ointment is new to the London and Dublin Pharmacopœias; it had a place in the Edinburgh. Use—in cutaneous ʼruptions.

Unguentum Creasoti.

It is twice the strength of the London, three times that of Edinburgh, and about the same as Dublin. Made with simple ointment, in place of lard.

Unguentum Elemi.

A different ointment to the London, the turpentine being left out, like the Dublin. It has one part of elemi to four of simple ointment.

Unguentum Gallæ.

This is the simple gall ointment of Dublin, having ten grains of powdered galls in (one drachm) the eighth part of an ounce.

Unguentum Gallæ cum Opio.

This ointment has one-fourth more galls, and twice as much opium as the London; one-third less galls, and only half the opium of the Edinburgh, the simple ointment of the P. B. being used instead of lard.

Unguentum Hydrargyri.

The same proportions are observed in this as in the ointment of the three previous Pharmacopœias.

Unguentum Hydrargyri Ammoniati.

This ointment is a third stronger than the corresponding ointment of London and Edinburgh.

Unguentum Hydrargyri Iodidi Rubri.

This ointment has only one-fourth the quantity of red iodide of mercury that the Dublin ointment had.

Unguentum Hydrargyri Nitratis.

This ointment is rather stronger than that of London, containing more of the nitrate of mercury, with an excess of acid. The form is that of Edinburgh, observing the same directions in making it. The acid solution of nitrate of mercury P.B. must not be used in making this ointment, as the proportions of acid and mercury are very different. The Dublin College directed equal parts of acid and mercury.

F

Unguentum Hydrargyri Oxidi Rubri.

Same strength as the ointment of the three previous Pharmacopœias.

Unguentum Iodi Compositum.

This ointment has the same quantity of iodine within two grains as London, Edinburgh, and Dublin, but only half the quantity of iodide of potassium.

Unguentum Plumbi Carbonatis.

This ointment resembles very closely the ointment of Edinburgh and Dublin.

Unguentum Plumbi Subacetatis.

This is the ceratum plumbi compositum of London, with white wax in place of yellow.

Unguentum Potassii Iodidi.

In this ointment the proportion of iodide of potassium is nearly the same as that of London and Dublin. It has eight grains of iodide of potassium in the eighth part of an ounce.

Unguentum Resinæ.

The proportions of this ointment are the same as those of Dublin, simple ointment P.B. being substituted for lard. It has about the same proportion of resin as the London cerate; it has rather less resin than the Edinburgh ointment.

Unguentum Sabinæ.

This ointment has the same strength of savin as the London. The time for digesting the savin in the melted wax and lard is now given (namely, twenty minutes); no time was before stated. In the Dublin ointment, the powdered savin was simply triturated with the ointment, and not strained out. It had one part in eight. The present has nearly the value of one part in two.

Unguentum Simplex.

This is a new form of simple ointment, composed of white wax, prepared lard, and almond-oil. It has a good consistence, and is a little more costly than prepared lard.

Unguentum Sulphuris.

As now prepared, is the same as Edinburgh and Dublin. It has only half the quantity of sulphur that the London ointment had.

Unguentum Terebinthinæ.

This ointment closely resembles the linimentum terebinthinæ of Edinburgh and Dublin.

Unguentum Veratriæ.

An addition to the Pharmacopœia ointments. It contains eight grains to the ounce. Used externally in neuralgia. It is often prescribed with as much as twice or thrice the quantity of veratria to the ounce.

Unguentum Zinci Oxidi.

The same proportions as the ointments of the three previous Pharmacopœias, using simple ointment in place of the lard of the London. The appearance of this ointment is improved by straining it, when melted and mixed, through a piece of muslin.

Veratria.

Is directed to be made according to the Edinburgh form, purifying as there ordered in an additional note.

Vinum Aloes.

Prepared according to the Edinburgh form. It has a fourth less aloes than the wine of the London Pharmacopœia, cardamoms and ginger taking the place of canella.

Vinum Antimoniale.

The same as London and Edinburgh. A fluid ounce should contain two grains of tartarated antimony.

Vinum Colchici.

Same proportions as London and Edinburgh, making up the full measure by additional sherry, after pressing and straining.

F 2

Vinum Ferri.

This wine is now directed to be made by dissolving tarta-rated iron in sherry. This is an improvement upon former wines of iron. It should contain eight grains in the fluid ounce. Dose—for children, a teaspoonful and upwards.

Vinum Ipecacuanhæ.

This wine has one-fifth less ipecacuanha than the wine of London, Edinburgh, and Dublin. One ounce contains the value of twenty-one grains of ipecacuanha.

Vinum Opii.

This wine is not now made with extract of opium, as the London, but with powdered opium, as the Dublin, omitting the cinnamon and cloves of London and Edinburgh. One fluid ounce should contain the value of thirty-two grains of powdered crude opium.

Zinci Acetas.

Acetic acid diluted with water, neutralized by carbonate of zinc with the aid of a gentle heat; then boiled for a few minutes, filtered, and set aside to crystallize; the mother liquor being decanted and evaporated, one-half fresh crystals will be formed, which may be added to the others, and both drained and dried in the usual way. Used as an eye lotion, in the proportion of two grains to the ounce of rose-water.

Zinci Carbonas.

Prepared by mixing solutions of carbonate of soda and sulphate of zinc; boiling the mixed solutions for fifteen minutes after effervescence has ceased, allowing the precipi-tate to subside, which should be well washed with repeated portions of boiling distilled water, and the precipitate col-lected and dried.

Zinci Chloridum.

A solution of granulated zinc in hydrochloric acid and dis-tilled water, purified by the addition of chlorine water and carbonate of zinc, subsequently filtered, evaporated, and cast in moulds. Used as a caustic; also as an injection in gonorrhœa, in the proportion of a grain to an ounce of water.

Zinci Oxidum.

Carbonate of zinc exposed to a dull red heat in a loosely-covered Hessian crucible. Used externally as a desiccative, by dusting, or in the form of ointment; internally, tonic and antispasmodic. Dose—one to five grains, in a pill.

Zinci Sulphas.

A solution of granulated zinc in sulphuric acid and distilled water, purified by the addition of chlorine water and carbonate of zinc, subsequently filtered, evaporated, and crystallized. Used externally as a lotion; in twenty-grain doses internally it acts as an emetic; in one or two grain doses two or three times a day, as an astringent and anti-convulsive.

Zinci Valerianas.

Prepared from solutions of valerianate of soda and sulphate of zinc, as directed in the Dublin Pharmacopœia. Tonic and antispasmodic. Dose—one to three grains, in a pill. These pills are less disagreeable when covered with a coating of tolu.

APPENDIX A.

*Contains a List of Articles employed in the Manufacture
of Preparations and Compounds used in Medicine.*

Acetate of Soda.

This salt is formed by dissolving carbonate of soda in acetic
acid, evaporating the solution, and setting the liquor aside to
crystallize; soluble in three parts of cold, in a less quantity of
boiling water, and in five of alcohol.

Æther, Pure.

Ordinary æther well washed with distilled water, and, after
separation, digested for twenty-four hours with recently-
burnt lime and chloride of calcium, then distilled by gentle
heat.

Arsenious Acid of Commerce.

Bichromate of Potash.

This salt is obtained by adding, in moderate quantity,
sulphuric, nitric, or acetic acid, to chromate of potash, one-
half of the base is removed, and the neutral chromate converted into bichromate. It is the more easily obtained by
using nitric or acetic acid, as the salt formed with these
acids is more readily separated than the sulphate, but sulphuric acid being cheaper, is more generally used.

Bismuth.

Is found chiefly in the metallic state, disseminated through
rocks, and is separated by exposure to heat.

Black Oxide of Manganese.

This is the commonest and most abundant ore of manganese.

Bone Ash.
The residue of ox and sheep bones, burned in contact with air, and reduced to powder.

Bone Black.
The residue of ox and sheep bones, burned out of contact with air, and reduced to powder.

Bread.
Made with wheaten flour.

Bromine.
Is manufactured from bittern, the mother-liquor of sea-water, from which the chloride of sodium has been separated by crystallization; it is also found in the Kreuznach Springs of Prussia, and exists in the salts of Kreuznach as imported into England, and used, dissolved in water, as an application to glandular swellings, in place of iodine and iodide of potassium.

Chalk.
The native friable carbonate of lime.

Chloride of Calcium.
The fused chloride of calcium.

Cotton.
Ordinary cotton wool of commerce.

Ferrocyanide of Potassium.
The yellow prussiate of potash. This salt, though harmless itself, is that from which hydrocyanic acid is obtained.

Flour.
Wheaten flour.

Fousel Oil.
Or fusel oil—amylic alcohol, obtained by further distillation from what remains in the still after the pure grain-spirit has been drawn off.

Hog's Fat.
The fat, commonly called flare.

Hydrochloric Acid of Commerce—Muriatic Acid.
Obtained commercially as a by-product by mixing sulphuric acid with chloride of sodium, being the first part of the process for the manufacture of carbonate of soda.

Iodine of Commerce.
Obtained from the ashes of marine plants.

Iron Wire.
Used in place of iron filings; should be free from rust.

Marble.
Hard white crystalline native carbonate of lime.

Mercury of Commerce—Quicksilver.
Obtained from the native sulphide of the mines.

Milk—Cow's Milk.

Nitrate of Potash of Commerce.
Nitre or saltpetre, a natural product, imported from the East Indies.

Nitrate of Soda.
A natural product, imported from Northern Chili; used in the preparation of nitric acid, also as a superficial manure by agriculturists; requires to be purified for chemical purposes.

Nitrite of Soda.
Nitrite of soda is now used in preparing the spiritus ætheris nitrosi: it is made in a similar way to nitrite of potash, by deflagrating in a Hessian crucible one part of recently-burnt and finely-powdered charcoal, and thirteen parts of nitrate of

soda, well mixed. When the deflagration is concluded, the crucible is covered, removed from the fire, and allowed to cool.

Ox Bile—Ox Gall.

The fresh bile of the ox : requires to be purified.

Phosphorus.

Is prepared from bones, is very inflammable, and requires great care, and is usually kept under water, being insoluble in it.

Pyroxylin—Gun Cotton.

The form given for this is more suitable for making explosive cotton than for the purpose of producing collodium or collodion for surgical use. The author has inserted a form with the notes upon collodium more adapted for the purpose.

Residue of Nitric Acid Process.

Bisulphate of potash or sal enixon.

Silver, Refined.

Pure metallic silver.

Solution of Persulphate of Iron.

Sulphate of iron brought to a state of persulphate by the action of nitric and sulphuric acids in solution in water.

Squirting Cucumber Fruit.

The nearly ripe fruit of ecbalium officinarum.

Sulphate of Ammonia.

Sulphate of Copper of Commerce.

Sulphate of Mercury.

Ten ounces of quicksilver of commerce and six fluid ounces of oil of vitriol are heated in a porcelain capsule until effervescence ceases, and nothing remains but a white, dry, crystalline salt.

Sulphuret of Antimony, Prepared.

Tersulphuret of antimony, "black antimony," reduced to powder.

Sulphuric Acid of Commerce.

Oil of vitriol, hydrated sulphuric acid.

Valerianate of Soda.

Take of bichromate of potash, in powder, nine ounces; fusel oil, four fluid ounces; oil of vitriol, six fluid ounces and a half; distilled water, half a gallon; solution of caustic soda, one pint, or as much as is sufficient. Dilute the oil of vitriol with ten ounces of water, and dissolve, with the aid of heat, the bichromate of potash in the remainder of the water. When both solutions have cooled down to nearly the temperature of the atmosphere, place them in a matrass, and having added the fusel oil, mix well by repeated shaking, until the temperature of the mixture has fallen to 80° or 90°. The matrass having been connected with a condenser, let heat be applied so as to distil over about half a gallon of liquid. Let this, when exactly saturated with the solution of caustic soda, be separated from a little oil that may float on its surface, and evaporated down until the escape of aqueous vapour having entirely ceased, the residual salt is liquefied. The heat should now be withdrawn, and when the valerianate of soda has concreted, it is, while warm, to be divided into fragments and preserved in a well-stoppered bottle. This is used in the preparation of valerianate of zinc, valerianate of iron, and valerianate of quinine.

Ferri Valerianas.

Take of valerianate of soda, five ounces and 180 grains; sulphate of iron, four ounces; distilled water, one pint. Let the sulphate of iron be converted into a persulphate, by the action of nitric and sulphuric acids, and by the addition of distilled water; let the solution of the persulphate be augmented to the bulk of eight fluid ounces. Dissolve the valerianate of soda in ten ounces of the water, then mix the two cold solutions, and having placed the precipitate which forms upon a filter and washed with the remainder of the water, let it be dried, by placing it for some days rolled in blotting-paper, on porous bricks. Dose—half a grain to one grain three times a day, in form of pill.

Quiniæ Valerianas.

Take of hydrochlorate of quinia, 420 grains.
   „   valerianate of soda .   124 grains.
   „   distilled water   .   16 ounces.

Dissolve the valerianate of soda in two ounces of the water, and the hydrochlorate of quinia in the remainder, and the temperature of each solution being raised to 120°, but not higher, let them be mixed, and let the mixture be set aside for twenty-four hours, when the valerianate of quinia will have become a mass of silky acicular crystals. Let these be pressed between folds of blotting-paper, and dried without the application of artificial heat. Dose—one to three grains as an antispasmodic tonic and antiperiodic in the form of pill three times a day. These two last preparations are not officinal, but, being frequently prescribed, it was thought desirable to place them here, as they have not been given with the valerianate of zinc among the Preparations and Compounds.

White of Egg.

The liquid albumen of the egg of the domestic fowl.

Zinc, Granulated.

Zinc granulated by fusing and pouring it from a height into cold water. The zinc here used should be zinc of commerce, purified.

Zinc of Commerce.

APPENDIX B.

Contains a List of Articles employed in Chemical Analysis, and Test Solutions for Qualitative and Volumetric Analysis.

Alcohol, Absolute Alcohol.

Pure or absolute alcohol may be obtained by re-distilling strong rectified spirit of commerce with half its weight of fresh quicklime.

Boracic Acid.

Chloride of Barium.

Copper Foil.

Pure metallic copper, thin and bright. Care should be taken that it is free from arsenic.

Ferridcyanide of Potassium.

Red prussiate of potash.

Gold, Fine.

Gold free from any metallic impurity.

Hyposulphite of Soda.

Indigo.

Isinglass.

Litmus.

Litmus Paper, Blue.

This paper may be conveniently and readily prepared as follows :—Take half an ounce of litmus cake, powder it and infuse with five ounces of boiling distilled water in a covered earthenware vessel for twelve hours, then pour off the clear liquor, straining through muslin ; take sheets of stout white blotting-paper, about ten inches long and four inches broad, stiffen the edge lengthways on one side by pasting on narrow strips of white cartridge paper ; now draw the sheets separately through the liquor placed in a shallow dish, and then hang them up to dry on lines of thick string, fastening by means of pegs or pins passed through the stiffened edges of the paper, and when dry cut into strips, and preserve out of contact of air and light.

Litmus Paper, Red.

Blue litmus paper dipped in distilled water slightly acidulated and dried.

Litmus Tincture.

This tincture should be made fresh when required, as it does not keep well.

Oxalic Acid of Commerce.

Oxalic Acid, Purified.

Dissolve oxalic acid in boiling distilled water ; filter the solution, and set aside to crystallize. This may be repeated, if necessary. It should leave no residue on ignition.

Plaster of Paris.

Platinum Foil.

Potassium.

Subacetate of Copper of Commerce.

Verdigris.

Sulphate of Copper, Anhydrous.

Sulphuret of Iron.

Sulphuretted Hydrogen.

Tin, Granulated.

Pure grain tin, granulated by fusing and pouring from a height into cold water.

Turmeric.

The rhizome of curcuma longa Linn.

Turmeric Paper.

May be prepared as litmus paper, using rather more turmeric.

Turmeric Tincture.

One ounce of bruised turmeric, macerated with six ounces of proof spirit for a week, and then filtered.

TEST SOLUTIONS FOR QUALITATIVE ANALYSIS.

Solution of Acetate of Copper.

Neutral acetate of copper dissolved in distilled water in the proportion of one part in ten, and filtered.

Solution of Acetate of Potash.

One part of acetate of potash dissolved in ten parts of distilled water, and filtered.

Solution of Acetate of Soda.

Prepared as solution of acetate of potash.

Solution of Albumen.

The white of one average-sized egg triturated with four ounces of distilled water and strained.

Solution of Ammonio-Nitrate of Silver.

Dissolve a quarter of an ounce of nitrate of silver in eight ounces of distilled water; into this solution, drop liquor of ammonia until the precipitate first formed is nearly dissolved, then filter the solution and make up the quantity to ten ounces with distilled water.

Solution of Ammonio - Sulphate of Copper.

This may be prepared in the same manner as the preceding solution, using half an ounce of sulphate of copper in the ten ounces of liquid.

Solution of Ammonio - Sulphate of Magnesia.

Dissolve half an ounce of sulphate of magnesia and a quarter of an ounce of hydrochlorate of ammonia in four fluid ounces of distilled water, and to the solution add two fluid drachms of solution of ammonia and as much distilled water as will make five fluid ounces, then filter.

Solution of Bichloride of Platinum.

The solution of the metal in nitro-hydrochloric acid, or aqua regia, is evaporated to dryness in a water-bath, and re-dissolved in ten parts of distilled water.

Solution of Boracic Acid.

Fifty grains of boracic acid, dissolved in one fluid ounce of rectified spirit.

Solution of Bromine.

Ten mimims of bromine and five fluid ounces of distilled water, shaken together in a well-stoppered bottle.

Solution of Carbonate of Ammonia.

Carbonate of ammonia dissolved in distilled water and filtered, in the proportion of one part of carbonate in ten of solution.

Solution of Chloride of Barium.

Crystals of chloride of barium, dissolved in distilled water in the proportion of one part in ten. The solution of these crystals should be neutral to test-papers, not affected by sulphuretted hydrogen, or hydrosulphuret of ammonia; it should leave no residue when mixed with excess of sulphuric acid filtered and evaporated.

Solution of Chloride of Calcium.

One part of chloride of calcium in ten parts of distilled water. The solution should be neutral.

Saturated Solution of Chloride of Calcium.

Solution of Chloride of Tin.

Prepared by boiling one ounce of granulated tin with three fluid ounces of hydrochloric acid diluted with one ounce of distilled water until gas is no longer given off; then adding as much distilled water as will make the quantity up to five fluid ounces. To be kept in a stoppered bottle, with some portions of metallic tin undissolved, to prevent the formation of any perchloride.

Solution of Corrosive Sublimate.

One hundred grains of corrosive sublimate dissolved in five ounces of distilled water.

Solution of Ferridcyanide of Potassium.

A quarter of an ounce of crystals of ferridcyanide of potassium dissolved in five fluid ounces of distilled water.

Solution of Ferrocyanide of Potassium.

A quarter of an ounce of crystals of ferrocyanide of potassium dissolved in five fluid ounces of distilled water.

Solution of Gelatine.

Isinglass dissolved in warm distilled water and strained.

Solution of Hydrochlorate of Ammonia.

One ounce of the hydrochlorate of ammonia in ten ounces of distilled water, and filtered.

Solution of Hydrosulphuret of Ammonia.

Is prepared by transmitting sulphuretted hydrogen gas through solution of ammonia till the liquid gives no precipitate with sulphate of magnesia. Should be kept in a well-stoppered bottle, free from lead. When first prepared, it is nearly colourless; but by keeping, it gradually assumes a yellow tint, which does not interfere with its action as a reagent.

Solution of Iodate of Potash.

Rub fifty grains of iodine with fifty grains of chlorate of potash, place the mixture in a Florence flask, and pour upon it half an ounce of water acidulated with ten minims of nitric acid, digest with gentle heat until the colour of iodine disappears. Boil for a minute, then transfer the contents to a porcelain capsule, and evaporate at 212° to perfect dryness; dissolve the residue in ten ounces of distilled water, and filter.

Solution of Iodide of Potassium.

One ounce of iodide of potassium in ten of the solution, in distilled water.

Solution of Oxalate of Ammonia.

Prepare oxalate of ammonia by slightly supersaturating a solution of pure oxalic acid with carbonate of ammonia and crystallizing. One part of this salt is then dissolved in forty parts of distilled water.

Solution of Phosphate of Soda.

Dissolve phosphate of soda in the proportion of one part in ten of distilled water.

Solution of Sulphate of Indigo.

Commercial indigo digested in sulphuric acid, and the solution diluted with distilled water until it is just distinctly blue.

Solution of Sulphate of Iron.

This solution should be freshly prepared by dissolving ten grains of pure sulphate of iron in a fluid ounce of distilled water.

G

Solution of Sulphate of Lime.

Add chloride of calcium to dilute sulphuric acid, and let the precipitate formed be well washed, digested, and agitated with distilled water, and the fluid filtered for use.

Solution of Tartaric Acid.

One ounce of crystals of tartaric acid dissolved in eight ounces of distilled water, and two fluid ounces of rectified spirit added.

Solution of Terchloride of Gold.

Take sixty grains of fine gold in a thin sheet, and place it in a flask with one fluid ounce of nitric acid and six fluid ounces of hydrochloric acid, previously mixed with four fluid ounces of distilled water, and digest until the gold is dissolved. Add to the solution one ounce more of hydrochloric acid, and evaporate at a heat not exceeding 212°, until acid vapours cease to come off, and dissolve the terchloride of gold thus formed in five fluid ounces of distilled water. In preparing these solutions, it is absolutely necessary, for obtaining satisfactory results, that the materials should be pure, and that in all cases, whether so stated or not, distilled water only should be used.

Test Solutions for Volumetric Analysis.

These solutions should contain, in a given volume, known quantities of an appropriate reagent, capable of producing a definite reaction with the substances to be estimated. It is also necessary that the value of the normal solutions should be accurately known, and that the alkalimeter tubes used should be uniform. Any one wishing to practise the volumetric system of analysis in its application to pharmacy, cannot do better than prepare the solutions according to the forms, as directed in the British Pharmacopœia, of which there are six, acknowledged to be a valuable addition to the work.

COX AND WYMAN, PRINTERS, GREAT QUEEN STREET, LONDON, W.C.

Breinigsville, PA USA
11 August 2010
243452BV00003B/44/P